MORE W

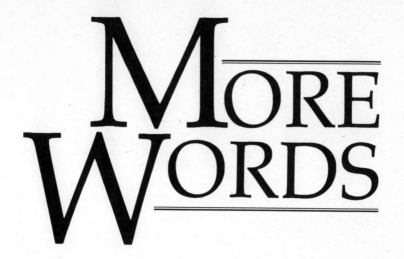

MORE WORDS

JOHN SILVERLIGHT

M

**MACMILLAN
PRESS**

in association with
THE OBSERVER

First published 1987

Published by
Higher and Further Education Division
MACMILLAN PUBLISHERS LTD
Houndmills, Basingstoke, Hampshire RG21 2XS
and London
Companies and representatives
throughout the world

Set in Palatino by Columns of Reading

Printed in Hong Kong

British Library Cataloguing in Publication Data
Silverlight, John
More words.
1. English language—Usage
I. Title
428.1   PE1460
ISBN 0-333-43683-0
ISBN 0-333-43684-9 Pbk

INTRODUCTION

The introduction to the first collection of *Words* columns from *The Observer* told how the feature originated and took shape. It contained, as is common, acknowledgments to people who had helped it develop – academics, lexicographers, colleagues, my family – and ended with thanks, 'most of all perhaps to readers of *The Observer*, who, almost from the start, have been responding to it, favourably, unfavourably, always helpfully'. This time readers are being thanked here, at the beginning of the introduction, with no 'perhaps' about the 'most of all'.

Reviewers of *Words* noticed the part readers had played in it. Mr D. J. Enright, in the *Listener*, wrote of the 'feeling of airiness and light' their letters brought 'to a physically small column of print'. Mr David Holloway, in the *Daily Telegraph*, said they gave 'a much more coherent shape to the book – a dialogue rather than a monologue'. What began as an optional, occasional light-hearted 'filler', intended to brighten the bottom of a page, has somehow converted itself, largely thanks to *Observer* readers, into a forum on usage, small in the numbers of people involved and the space in the paper it takes up, but not in range or learning. On matters that are out of my ken – the classics, say, or scientific matters or lexicography – I try to keep in touch with experts. Sometimes I get what they say wrong, or try to compress too much information into too confined a space. Distortion creeps in, if not downright error. On such occasions, as I prepare to wear a white sheet, I think wryly of how gratifying, if daunting, it is to have so informed a readership – see, for example, 'Celsius/Centigrade' and 'Egregious' in the following pages. (The American columnist William Safire also makes effective use of readers' letters in his book *On Language*, based on his column of the same title in the *New York Times* magazine. The book, which is wholly admirable, has sadly not been published in this country, but the column is syndicated in the *New York Herald Tribune*.)

There is the ideal reader's letter. It makes a new point or develops one that I have made rather than just correcting me on something. It needs little or no editing. It is just long enough to allow space for me to say who the writer is and what he or she is writing about and to add a sentence or two in order to justify my signing the piece. (After varying considerably in length from week to week, the column has settled down, at least for the time being, to about 260 words.) There have been one or two such letters over the years; to hope for more would be unrealistic. More numerous are letters with a question on usage or derivation which, on my looking into it in order to reply, produces such interesting information that suddenly a piece is conceived; birth is often more difficult. There are letters with questions that do not produce a column yet involve a lot of work to produce a reply. That is part of the job – and often I learn something useful from the work. And there are letters from readers who merely wish to share a thought with someone they think might be interested. All those categories are rewarding.

But inevitably there are letters that are more difficult to deal with. These are mainly from readers who believe that our language is dangerously in decline and that it is my duty to campaign against bad usage in general and, in particular, whatever example of such usage it is that they object to. My generally permissive attitude is not popular. One reader, apropos my defence of 'target' as a verb, wrote that no such verb appeared in his 1905 edition of Nuttall's dictionary. He added: 'The sloppy practice, mainly by journalists, of using nouns as verbs is to be deplored.' I replied that the OED had an example of 'target' as a verb dated 1837. Less easy to answer was a letter about my agreeing, regretfully, that the distinction between 'shall' and 'will' was dying. 'A self-respecting journal', the correspondent wrote, 'would be heading the attack upon loose language, not simply observing its decline.' In the end I wrote, and I meant it, that it was good to hear from someone who so clearly cared about the language. Such people do care deeply and passionately about it, but although I am not out of sympathy with them, I am in complete disagreement with their assumptions (1) that the language is in decline and (2) that any of us, or at any rate most of us, can do anything to 'improve' or 'disimprove' it. I know of no instance of a successful campaign against 'incorrect' usage. As Mrs Lesley Burnett of the Oxford English Dictionaries says, 'If it's reached the stage of people shouting about it, it's too late to do anything about it.'

As for 'improving' the language, the great Danish linguist Otto Jespersen (1860–1943) does cite an example in his *Growth and Structure of the English Language*, first published 1905. Writing of

Shakespeare's 'boldness in regard to words' he says: 'In turning over the pages of the New English Dictionary [as the OED was first entitled], where every pain has been taken to ascertain the earliest occurrence of each word . . . one is struck by the frequency with which Shakespeare's name is affixed to the earliest quotation'. Examples include 'aslant' as a preposition: 'There is a willow grows aslant a brook' (*Hamlet*); 'assassination': 'If it were done when 'tis done, then 'twere well/It were done quickly; if the assassination/Could trammel up the consequence, and catch/With his surcease success' (*Macbeth*); 'dwindle': 'Bardolph, am I not fallen away vilely since this last action? do I not bate? do I not dwindle?' (*1 Henry IV*); 'laughable'; 'lonely'. Nouns used as verbs? The earliest quotation of 'bound' in the sense of 'spring upward' is 'He leaps, he neighs, he bounds' (*Venus and Adonis*) – I wish I had remembered that one when replying to the correspondent who deplored the 'sloppy practice, mainly by journalists' etc. The earliest quotation of 'excellent' in the current sense of 'extremely good' is ''Fore God, an excellent song' (*Othello*). (Extracts taken from the tenth edition, 1982, Basil Blackwell.)

Not, of course, that Shakespeare necessarily coined those words. His being quoted so often, Jespersen says, 'is due in many cases to the fact that his vocabulary has been registered with greater care in concordances'. That will not happen to most of us. All we can do is try to speak and write as clearly as we can, which is worth doing anyway, whether or not it 'improves' the language. Arthur Quiller-Couch, in *The Art of Writing*, his first course of lectures in 1913–14 as King Edward Professor of English Literature at Cambridge, quotes a French writer – not named – as saying, '*la clarté est la politesse*'.

Language is a mystery. That is one of the three things I know about it. Dr Robert Burchfield writes in *The English Language* (Oxford University Press):

The origin of language is unknown and all theories about this problem are spurious. No languageless human society has ever been discovered on the earth. The faculty of speech therefore precedes recorded history and it is unhelpful to speculate about the circumstances of its origin. The doctrine of Hobbes, and of many Christians, that 'all this language gotten, and augmented by Adam and his posterity, was again lost at the tower of Babel, when by the hand of God, every man was stricken for his rebellion, with an oblivion of his former language' is an engaging but unacceptable myth.

I know too that language is very powerful, far more powerful than the people who use it. According to George Steiner in his *After Babel* (OUP), the French biologist Jacques Monod has said that language

> may have appeared in pre-humans . . . But once it had come into even rudimentary existence, language was bound to confer an immensely increased selective value on the capacity for recording and for symbolic combination. 'In this hypothesis, language may have preceded, perhaps by some time, the emergence of a central nervous system particular to man and have contributed decisively to the selection of those variants aptest to utilise all its resources. In other words, language may have created man, rather than man language.'

And I know that language is in constant process of change. There are those who feel that, whereas in the past change was slow and measured, in this century it has been – is being – swift and violent. D. J. Enright once wrote in a letter to the Editor commenting on my describing myself as 'impenitently permissive': 'What we have now is not so much linguistic development as a series of jolts – imposition rather than selection by the test of time. The difference might be compared to war by bow-and-arrow (which, obviously, the race has survived) and nuclear war (which could jolt us to pieces).'

Against this, Dr Burchfield writes in his book of earlier 'remarkable and irreversible changes' (he describes them elsewhere as 'more grievous or more fundamental') that have come upon the English language since the Old English period. They include the loss of grammatical gender; the great vowel shift of the fifteenth century, 'when nearly every long vowel sound in the standard language radically changed its nature' ('goose', for instance, had formerly rhymed with 'close', 'house' with 'moose'); the abandonment of dual forms of pronouns (such as 'thee' and 'you'); the decay of the subjunctive. Here is William Caxton writing in 1490, near the end of his life:

> And certaynly our langage now vsed varyeth ferre from that which was vsed and spoken when I was borne. For we englysshemen ben borne vnder the domynacyon of the mone, which is neuer steadfaste but euer wauerynge wexynge one season and waneth and dycreaseth another season.

This passage is quoted in *Language Change: Progress or Decay?* by Jean Aitchison, Fontana Paperbacks. Dr Johnson, prescriptivist at heart though he was, accepted the inevitability of change. He writes in the preface of his *Dictionary of the English Language*:

> The tropes of poetry will make hourly encroachments, and the metaphorical will become the current sense: pronunciation will be varied by levity or ignorance, and the pen must at length comply with the tongue.

That is the point: in the end the spoken word will prevail. We were talking many, many thousands of years before we were writing. And, in Johnson's superb image,

> sounds are too volatile and subtle [both words rhymed with 'pencil' in his day] for legal restraints; to enchain syllables, and to lash the wind, are equally the undertaking of pride, unwilling to measure its desires by its strength.

Miss Aitchison, answering the question in the subtitle of her book just mentioned, writes:

> Once we have stripped away religious and philosophical preconceptions, there is no evidence that language is either progressing or decaying. Disruption and therapy seem to balance one another in a perpetual stalemate. These two opposing pulls are an essential characteristic of language.

For myself, permissive or not, I do not promise never to protest against what I see as trends I disapprove of; there are examples in this book. That may be inconsistent, but I also agree with the American poet John Ciardi, quoted in the Harper Dictionary of Contemporary Usage:

> Are there any enduring standards of English usage? I think there are only preferences, 'passionate preferences', as Robert Frost used to say. . . In the long run the usage of those who do not think about the language will prevail. It is worth remembering that Swift inveighed against 'mob' as a vulgar corruption of *mobile vulgus* . . . It will not do to resist uncompromisingly. Yet those who care have a duty to resist. Changes that occur against such resistance are tested changes. The language is the better for them – and for the resistance.

So, the word is not 'campaign' or 'attack' or 'fight'. It is resistance.

A word of gratitude to five more people: Mrs Lesley Burnett, who is quoted earlier and is revising the Shorter Oxford Dictionary; two classical scholars, the historian

Mr C. M. Woodhouse and the publisher Mr Colin Haycraft; and two *Observer* writers, Mr Anthony Howard, the Deputy Editor, who was largely responsible for the continuance of the column after my retirement as an Assistant Editor in 1984, and Mr William Millinship, Managing Editor, who deals with my articles from week to week.

ACQUAINTANCE.

For some time I have been trying to avoid using the word 'friend' (see entry) too loosely, bearing in mind the Concise Oxford definition, 'One joined to another in intimacy and mutual benevolence.' But 'acquaintance' often will not do either: 'knowledge more than mere recognition and usually less than intimacy . . . 2, person with whom one is acquainted' (Concise Oxford); 'person whom one knows but is not a particularly close friend' (Longman's Dictionary of the English Language); 'knowledge especially falling short of intimacy; person known slightly' (Chambers). Webster's New Dictionary of Synonyms says both words 'imply a degree of familiarity, "friend" distinctively connoting close bonds of love and affection, and "acquaintance" comparative infrequency of contact and less close personal interest: "You understand I am not their friend. I am only a holiday acquaintance" – Conrad.'

There are people I know for whom neither word will do. Take a professional contact, an academic, say, or publisher, whom I frequently consult. We lunch together once a year, perhaps twice; we have not been to each other's houses; if he or she is married our spouses haven't met. Yet I enjoy that person's company as much as that of any friend or relation, more in some cases. With all due diffidence, the feeling seems mutual. 'Friend' is too strong, 'acquaintance' not strong enough. Edmund Blunden wrote of a similar problem in his poem *The Hill*: 'Praise is not safe, description will not do.'

'Crony' ('Jack Cole, my old schoolfellow . . . who was a great chrony of mine' – Pepys) is as unhelpful as any other synonym of 'friend' – 'chum', 'pal' etc. – but I like the derivation: from Greek *chronios*, long-standing, from *chronos*, time.

28 SEPTEMBER 1986

AFTERMATH.

Mr Lawrence Young, of Sparkford in Somerset, writes apropos a caption in *The Observer*, 'The aftermath of the first atom bomb', under a photograph of Hiroshima in 1945: 'I have noticed before that the word "aftermath" is used as if it meant the consequences of some destructive action whereas according to dictionaries it means a second crop mowed in the same season.' That is indeed the first sense given in the Oxford English Dictionary: -*math* comes

1

from an old Teutonic root meaning to mow. However 'aftermath' also has the extended figurative sense of consequence and even of 'period immediately following a usually disastrous event', as in 'the aftermath of the war' – Webster's Collegiate Dictionary. The OED quotes Hartley Coleridge (son of the poet) in an example dated 1851: 'The aftermath of the great rebellion'. I did not know of the agricultural sense, which I think must be obsolescent, at least in general use. Now, thanks to Mr Young, I am aware of the immense power of the metaphor in the figurative sense.

13 MAY 1984

Berriew, Powys

DEAR JOHN SILVERLIGHT, *You must mix only with arable farmers not to know the agricultural meaning of 'aftermath'. In all the West and Wales the term is in daily use and, with the new EEC policies for milk, the prosperity of many farmers in the next year will depend on their ability to make good silage from the aftermath (if the present weather continues there will not be any aftermath).*

I shall be surprised if you do not have a host of letters of surprise that you do not know the origin of the word.

Yours sincerely

D. W. SMITH

'Host of letters' is quite right. My friend Mrs Mary Large, who farms in the east of England (near Lincoln), where farms are indeed largely arable, told me that the usual term there is 'second cut'. But if beasts are put on a field immediately after the first cut, the expression is 'putting them on the aftermath'. Mr Harold Peart, of Stannington in Northumberland, wrote: 'I was brought up between the wars on a hill farm in the north of England; summers were too late and too short to permit a second cut of grass, but after the first cut had been taken the aftermath was always used for grazing animals. We did use the term "aftermath" for the second growth, but more often we referred to it as "fog". I have always assumed this to be a dialect word but, somewhat to my surprise, I have found it in the OED ("of unknown origin") with half a column of definitions (basically "the aftermath") and examples of its use.

Other words derived from it include the legal term "foggage", the privilege of pasturing cattle on fog.' (By a nice coincidence, shortly after I received Mr Peart's letter my elder son showed me a copy of 'Horticulturist and Seedsman John Chambers' Catalogue with Wild Flower Gardening Information'. One of the items available was 'Yorkshire fog, *Holcus lanatus*'.)

Mrs C. M. Thompson of Solihull wrote that in south-west Herefordshire, where she was brought up on a small farm, 'the term for second cut was (and still is) "lattermath". Try saying it out loud – it's a lovely sound!' Mr T. Bolton, of Orrell near Wigan, had not encountered 'aftermath' until reading the *Words* piece. 'Less than twelve hours later, rereading Robert Louis Stevenson's *Travels with a Donkey in the Cevennes*, I came upon: "Pradelles stands on a hillside, high above the Allier, surrounded by rich meadows. They were cutting aftermath on all sides, which gave the neighbourhood, this gusty autumn morning, an untimely smell of hay."' And Mr Paul Abbott of Cambridge, enclosing a copy of Edward Thomas's poem *It was Upon*, wrote: 'As you will see, in its first occurrence the word "lattermath" has its agricultural meaning; by its second appearance the word has been poetically transformed to give it the metaphorical, more usual sense.'

> It was upon a July evening.
> At a stile I stood, looking along a path
> Over the country by a second Spring
> Drenched perfect green again. 'The lattermath
> will be a fine one.' So the stranger said,
> A wandering man. Albeit I stood at rest,
> Flushed with desire I was. The earth outspread,
> Like meadows of the future I possessed.
>
> And as an unaccomplished prophecy
> The stranger's words, after the interval
> Of a score years, when those fields are by me
> Never to be recrossed, now I recall,
> This July eve, and question, wondering,
> What of the lattermath to this hoar Spring?

That poem was written in 1916. At 7.36 on the morning of 9 April 1917, in the first hour of the Arras offensive, Thomas was killed by the blast of a shell in his forward observation post.

A̲GENDA. Mr Ian Barnish of Ramsgate quotes *The Observer*'s Pendennis diarist as writing, 'For a start, the agenda contains . . . '. 'If the author of the diary', he goes on, 'read *Words*, he would know that "agenda" is the plural of *agendum* and cannot be followed by a verb in the singular.'

I fear that Mr Barnish's faith in me is misplaced: I too would have written 'contains'. As Mr Michael McCrum, Master of Corpus Christi College, Cambridge, and a classical scholar, has observed in this column, 'agenda' as a singular 'has been almost wholly acclimatised'. Fowler's *Modern English Usage*, in the second edition revised by Sir Ernest Gowers and first published in 1965, has: 'Although *agenda* is a plural word, it is pedantry to object to the common and convenient practice of treating it as a singular one.'

Apropos plurals my lexicographer friend John Ayto has found this sentence in *A Little Learning*, the autobiography of Evelyn Waugh, 'a noted precisian in matters of style: "My brother was home by Christmas and that holidays were the most joyous of my life."' Is 'holidays' singular or plural, Mr Ayto asks, and he quotes Robert Southey, writing in 1825: 'Blair spent one summer holidays with his mother'. Waugh could not quite bring himself to do that, Mr Ayto says, 'but he was evidently in some doubt'. He also quotes examples of some of 'these curious singular/plural nouns that have become unambiguously established as the term for an individual entity, e.g. "waxworks", "forceps" and "barracks"', so taking a singular verb.

Another plural whose 'fate to be singular', Mr McCrum said in June, 'is perhaps sealed' is 'media'. I shall go on resisting this in order to assert the diverse idea, but it looks like a losing, if not a lost, cause. I am reliably told that the French have already sold out and often refer to '*les médias*'.

8 APRIL 1984

A̲LFS, OCKERS AND ROYS. Mr Peter Hayes, of Greymouth in New Zealand, sends us a cutting from a local paper about a traveller in Brisbane who found that the domestic flight he hoped to take was full. A notice said: 'Sorry. Ocker Fokker chocker.' Fokker was obviously a plane – could we supply the other derivations? In this country 'chocker', from 'chock-a-block', means fed up. In Australian slang, says Collins, it means full.

'Ocker', according to the latest edition of Partridge's *Dictionary of Slang and Unconventional English* (1984), edited by Paul Beale, means 'a constant disparager, whose assurance matches his ignorance and prejudice; "the uncultivated Australian" (G. A. Wilkes, *A Dictionary of Australian Colloquialisms*, 1978).' In the appendix Mr Beale writes: 'It derives, I believe, from "knocker", an inveterate adverse-criticiser: "a knocker" has become "an 'ocker" by a well-known phonetic process: in originally careless pronunciation, "knocker" = "nocker", therefore "a nocker" becomes "an ocker", and the noun is apprehended as "ocker"; cf. "a nadder" (Middle English *naddre*), which duly became "an adder".' 'Ocker' is a synonym of the earlier 'Alf', 'which has fallen out of favour because of the English TV character Alf Garnett, who has some but not all of the characteristics of the Australian "Alf".'

The opposite of 'Alf' is the trendy, middle-class 'Roy'. Murray Sayle, writing in *Encounter* of May 1960, refers to 'the Australian businessman or big landowner, the button-down shirt, lightweight-suit type of smoothie from the North Shore Line in Sydney or Toorak Road in Melbourne, with his spurious "taste" and "culture" (a hasty warm-up of European and American leftovers) . . . In current Australian terminology, this is the "Roy" type . . . '

Mr Sayle clearly felt closer to the Australian worker, 'the "Alf" as we call him . . . Hardly another country in the world has a working class so free of inferiority feelings, or worse, inverted working-class snobbery; so determined to get his share of any prosperity that is going; so impervious to the subjugating tricks of accent, style and spurious patriotism used by practically every ruling class in the world. Alf may be ignorant, but he and his mates are freer, more resistant to exploitation than the bottom people of any other country . . . Alf's militant ignorance is one of his most powerful defences, his contempt for "bullshit" protects him against the browbeating so readily used by the boss-class of Britain and the Eastern, industrial side of the United States, whose class-demarcating "education" and manners can be bought by anyone with the money to be spent at public or (in the US) private schools.'

Mr Sayle's article also explains something that has puzzled

me ever since I first heard the words of 'Waltzing Matilda'. Why was the song's lowly (as I thought) squatter 'mounted on his thorough-bred' and accompanied by 'his troopers, one-two-three'? When Australia began to be carved up on a grand scale, Mr Sayle writes, 'the land-takers had no legal rights: they squatted, and so we call a great landowner a squatter'.

3 MARCH 1985

A LLEGORY. B. R. Ariel of East Finchley, London, writes: 'I have always been at a loss to explain the difference between (1) allegory and parable and (2) parody and pastiche.' I was about to dash off an explanation, only to realise that I was at a loss too.

'Allegory' and 'parable', says Fowler, 'are almost interchangeable. Usage, however, has decided that "parable" is the fitter name for the illustrative story [e.g. the parable of the Good Samaritan] designed to suggest a single principle, and offer a definite moral, while "allegory" is to be preferred when the purpose is less exclusively didactic and the story of greater length [e.g. *The Faerie Queen*] . . . The object of a parable is to persuade or convince; that of an allegory is often rather to please. But the difference is not inherent in the words themselves; it is a result of their history, the most important factor being the use of "parable" to denote the allegorical stories told by Christ.'

'Parody', 'burlesque', 'caricature' and 'travesty', Fowler says, are often interchangeable; all four could be applied to a badly conducted trial. But the first three also have each a special province: action or acting is burlesqued, form and feature are caricatured, and verbal expression is parodied. '"Travesty" has no special province and is more used than the others when the imitation is intended to be an exact one and fails.'

'Pastiche', in contrast, is not a mocking word. It means 'medley, esp. musical composition, or picture, made up from various sources; literary or other work of art composed in the style of a well-known author' – Concise Oxford. It derives from Italian *pasta*, one sense of which is a hard, brilliant glass used in making imitation gems. I have heard *Der Rosenkavalier* described as pastiche and, much as I love Strauss in general and *Rosenkavalier* in particular, I would agree. Pastiche cannot produce great art, but it can give great pleasure and produce very fine art indeed.

5 OCTOBER 1986

A POSTROPHE. In his wholly admirable book *The English Language*, published last January, Dr Robert Burchfield writes: 'The prevalence of incorrect instances of the use of the apostrophe at the present time, even in the work of otherwise reasonably well-educated people (e.g. it's wings, apple's for sale, this is your's), together with the abandonment of it by many business firms (Barclays Bank, Lloyds Bank), suggest that the time is close at hand when this moderately useful device should be abandoned.' This, Kingsley Amis prophesied gloomily in a generally favourable review in this paper, would loose 'a flood of ambiguity'.

I like the advertisement I saw in the Tube saying that 'British Rail Property Board is busy refurbishing its' arches'. Not that I can crow. Thanks to a typing error, the phrase 'One of the last monarch's to wash the feet of the [Maundy money] recipients . . . ' appeared in *Words* on 31 March (see MAUNDY; the intrusive apostrophe has been removed). Mrs Jean Elliott, of Upminster in Essex, wrote that it quite spoilt her Sunday morning. Abject apologies. Mrs Elliot enclosed another *Observer* cutting with two examples of 'your's' and asked, 'Isn't it time we abandoned apostrophes altogether?'

No, not in elisions. I would deprecate the replacement of, say, 'I'll be seeing you' by 'Ill [or 'shell' or 'hell' or 'well'] be seeing you'. Possessives are another matter. Take the uneasy history of the possessive of 'it'. 'It's' appears in books just before 1600, says the OED. But 'its' was appearing too, if less often, and 200 years later the apostrophe had disappeared, apparently without causing confusion or ambiguity. I think they could all go now, with one exception: Queens' College, Cambridge. I once saw a reference in the *Observer Magazine* to 'Sir Eric Ashby, Provost of Queen's'. Sir Eric (now Lord Ashby) was actually *Master of Clare*, and Queens' has a *President*. But what irritated me most was the misplaced apostrophe. The college (my college) was founded in 1448 by Margaret of Anjou, wife of Henry VI, and again in 1475 by Elizabeth Woodville, wife of Edward IV. Two queens.

12 MAY 1984

Letters of protest against my dismissive attitude towards the apostrophe poured in. This was predictable, understandable and wholly praiseworthy. It is good that people who care about the language should express themselves forcibly. I also had to write and apologise to several readers for my overlooking the fact that Lord Ashby had been President and Vice-Chancellor of Queen's University, Belfast, 1950–59 and was still its Chancellor.

A PRIL. This article was meant to explore the origins of April Fool's Day, but all I found was familiar speculation and little fresh fact. 'April' quotations were more worthwhile: Chaucer's 'Aprille with hise schoures swote', of course; Shakespeare's 'The uncertain glory of an April day' (*Two Gentlemen of Verona*). What a shock Eliot's *The Waste Land* must have been in 1922:

> April is the cruellest month, breeding
> Lilacs out of the dead land, mixing
> Memory and desire, stirring
> Dull roots with spring rain.

But what really struck me was a 1940 cutting from the *Liverpool Post* to the effect that in 1564 the French adopted 1 January as the start of the year rather than 1 April. It wasn't quite right, but a little research produced some fascinating information.

In Julius Caesar's calendar the year began on 1 January, which continued in general use for some centuries; the church, it seems, put up with it because of its proximity to Christmas. Then 25 March, Lady Day, began to take over. It seemed more logical, according to the 'Handbook of Dates for Students of English History' (Royal Historical Society, 1945), to start the year with the Feast of the Annunciation (which commemorates Gabriel's announcement to the Virgin of the Incarnation and the conception of Christ in her womb) rather 'than with the Feast of the Nativity'. Things got so confused, says the book, that someone travelling from Venice on 1 March 1245 would find himself, in Florence, in 1244 and, going on to Pisa, in 1246. England plumped for 1 January in 1752 (Scotland did so in 1600) in accordance with an Act which also decreed the adoption of the Gregorian calendar: after 2 September eleven days were omitted, making the ensuing day 14 September – mobs charged through the streets chanting, 'Give us back our eleven days!' That is why the financial year begins on 5 April, which would be the 'correct' date of Lady Day had its date not remained, much to my satisfaction, Old Style.

1 APRIL 1984

A═══ UGUST.

By 28 BC, 17 strife-torn years after the assassination of Julius Caesar, his niece's son Octavian stood out as the only hope of peace for his fellow Romans. He was now supreme and he was looking for another name in order, as the *Cambridge Ancient History* has it, to raise him 'in some degree above ordinary human standards' – half a century earlier the dictator Sulla had named himself Fortunate (*Felix*) and had conferred the name Great on his lieutenant Pompey. Octavian considered the name Romulus, founder of Rome, and rejected it because Romulus was a king: although Octavian was absolute master, he was also at pains to foster the illusion that he was preserving the Republic and, as *Everyman's Encyclopaedia* has it, 'carefully avoided all forms, titles and honours suggestive of kingly power'.

He came up with *Augustus*, majestic, worthy of honour, and in January 27 BC a grateful Senate bestowed the name upon him. A further resolution changed the name of the month Sextilis to Augustus, just as the month Quintilis had given way to Julius, when Caesar reformed the calendar. Those two resolutions have kept his name alive ever since – I know of only two languages that do not use the word 'August' or a derivative: Czech, which has *srpen*, sickle, symbol of harvest, and Polish, *sierpień*.

4 AUGUST 1985

Readers were quick to inform me about other languages that do not use 'August' or a derivative. They include Irish (*Lunasa*, after Lugh, Celtic god of genius and light), Lithuanian (*rugpiutis*, rye harvest), Finnish (*elokuu*, month of harvest), Croat (*kolovoz*, to drive a cart).

A═══ UTHORITY.

A *Times* obituary headline on 27 April read: 'Professor A. C. Gimson, authority on the pronunciation of

English'. It was appropriate. In the early days of this column, when I was tentatively feeling my way on practically everything, I had the good fortune of getting to know Professor Gimson ('Gim' to his friends), head of the Department of Phonetics at University College, London, and editor of Everyman's English Pronouncing Dictionary, the 'bible' in the pronunciation business. From then on, in one area at least, I had no more worries. Certainty in matters of usage is unattainable. True authority is rare but can be found. 'Gim' had it with his open, inquiring mind, dedicated to the search for truth. I shall miss him, personally as much as professionally.

26 MAY 1985

AUTUMN. Tomorrow is the Autumnal Equinox, one of the two moments in the year (the other is the Vernal Equinox) when the sun crosses the equator and days are equal to nights all over the world. That, indeed, is why the equator is so called.

'Autumn', says the OED, is from the Latin *autumnus*, 'also written *auctumnus*, of doubtful etymology. See Lewis and Short.' I had always taken for granted that 'autumn' derived from *augeo*, to increase, with its past participle *auctus*, plentiful, abundant. Lewis and Short, however, have '*auctumnus*, correctly *autumnus* . . . was originally referred to *augeo*, as the season of increase'. Later scholars, however, 'refer it to the Sanscrit *av*, to do good to, to satisfy oneself' . . . thus 'the season of abundance'. Whatever the etymology, it has produced two of the loveliest words in our language.

Autumn, like spring, has a reputation for storminess. According to the scholar and critic Richard Bentley (1662–1742), 'The months of March and September, the two aequinoxes of our year, are the most tempestuous.' One OED definition of 'equinoctial' reads, 'Happening at or near to the time of the equinox; said especially of the "gales" prevailing about the time of the autumnal equinox', and Livingstone, in his *Narrative of an Expedition to the Zambesi*, wrote, 'the equinoctial gales made it impossible for us to cross to the eastern side'. All this clashed with my feeling of a sense of repose in 'autumn' and 'autumnal', so I was pleased to learn from *Everyman's Encyclopaedia* that 'equinoctial gales' are 'a popular superstition.

10

Storms are not more prevalent at the equinoxes than at other seasons.' One of Donne's most beautiful Elegies begins,

> No *Spring* nor *Summer* Beauty hath such grace,
> As I have seen in one *Autumnall* face.

In one of his sermons he said: 'In heaven it is always Autumn; his mercies are ever in the maturity.'

22 SEPTEMBER 1985

BLACK/WHITE.

Are there two words more starkly opposed than 'black' and 'white'? 'White: Free from malignity or evil intent, esp. as opposed to something characterised as "black"'– OED. It's not just in English. In French *blancheur* can also mean purity, innocence; *noirceur* can mean heinousness, baseness, atrocity, treacherous action. German has its equivalents; so, no doubt, do other languages. Horace writes in his *Satires*: 'That man is black at heart, mark and avoid him, if you are a true Roman.' The king's beloved in the Song of Solomon proclaims: 'I am black but comely, O ye daughters of Jerusalem.' Why the 'but'?

An obsolete sense of 'white' is 'fair-seeming'; 'whites' is a 'popular name for leucorrhoea, or "white flux"' (OED); there is 'whited sepulchre'– three unpleasant associations, but I had to look for them. In contrast, black art or magic, blackball, black looks (and books), black cap (still a chilling memory), blackguard, blackleg, black list and blackmail come to mind effortlessly. Most uncomfortable nowadays is the concept of the 'White Man' as '(colloq.) person of honourable character, good breeding etc.' – Concise Oxford; most desk dictionaries have something similar. Much as I enjoy Kipling, I gag at 'An' for all 'is dirty 'ide/'E was white, clear white inside' (cf. Blake's 'And I am black, but O! my soul is white').

So, is language racist? Yes, and sexist. 'Virtue' derives ultimately from Latin *vir*, man. And class-ridden. 'Peasant', at one time denoting a respectable calling, has been derogatory for centuries; 'villain', equally respectable, has fared even worse. One comforting thought. A classical scholar says that notwithstanding the Horace quotation above, Romans – and Greeks, for that matter – did not suffer from racial prejudice.

17 NOVEMBER 1985

11

The Polytechnic of North London
Department of Language and Literature

DEAR MR SILVERLIGHT, *'And I am black, but O! my soul is white'* – are you suggesting that Blake was an unwitting racist? Reading this poem (The Little Black Boy) in the context of his *Songs*, most students of Blake would today, I think, take these as the words of a black child who, through the agency of his loving but naïve mother, has been indoctrinated with the pernicious beliefs that further the ends of his white exploiters. In Blake's writings 'white' nearly always carries unpleasant associations.

Yours sincerely

GEOFFREY JACKSON

Mr Jackson is quite right; I should have made the point clear. Professor Peter Campbell, of the Department of Politics at Reading University, sent me a photocopy of an article in *The Times Higher Educational Supplement* of 12 November 1982 by Linda Hall, senior lecturer in English and Professional Studies at the Bulmershe College of Higher Education, attacking the idea that the unfavourable connotations of 'black' are the product of a 'colonial and imperialist past'. Most of the phrases involving the word 'black', she says, 'were with us long before the Empire took shape and even before the slave trade began'. 'Blackguard', for instance, 'appears in the Middle Ages as an ironic term for the scullery lads who looked after the pots and pans in the royal and noble kitchens. The lowly *social* connotations of a neutral job description became associated – by a no less insidious shift – with moral inferiority, possibly because it would be a perfect term of abuse for one member of the gentry to fling at another.

'"Blackleg", first recorded in 1722, was originally a disease of sheep and cattle which caused the legs of animals to turn black. As it was an infectious disease, affected animals were kept isolated. First-generation industrial workers would have had little difficulty recalling their agricultural origins. As for the sense of disgrace associated with being in someone's "black books", it is Roman Catholics who have cause to complain rather than people of African origin. Though the term started out quite simply as an official book bound in black during the reign of Edward III (1327–77), it took on its metaphorical sense of disfavour only after Henry VIII's commissioners had used such books to record the abuses uncovered in the monasteries prior to the Dissolution.'

The article ends, 'We need not see in these terms any insult to black *people* . . . This kind of linguistic sensitivity only serves to drive a wedge between the races and to destroy any chance of a genuinely harmonious multi-ethnic society.' All very salutory, not to say etymologically fascinating. Hyper-sensitivity is to be discouraged. But I still do not think it does any harm at least to be conscious of those 'unfavourable connotations'.

It was gratifying that most of the letters, even those correcting me on points of detail, expressed sympathy with the general idea. One such detail was my remark that 'Romans and Greeks did not suffer from racial prejudice'. Mr Edward Murray-Harvey of Hellesdon-next-Norwich commented, 'As they were the ruling races, I am sure they did not. Was the meaning that the Romans and Greeks did not *practise* racial prejudice?' While I agree that 'practise' would have been clearer, I don't altogether regret 'suffer', ambiguous though it was. Racial prejudice is a disease.

BOORS, BORES & CO. 'He thinks I'm a bore and I think he's a boor.' My reaction to this 'overhear' (I owe the term to my *Observer* colleague Alan Watkins) was: What a nice example of a doublet, a pair of words derived from the same source but different in meaning and spelling, e.g. 'discreet' and 'discrete', 'cloak' and 'clock'. I was wrong. 'Bore' and its verb, says the OED, 'arose about 1750; etymology unknown'. 'Boor' may have been native English in the sixteenth century, 'representing a shortening of Old English *gebúr*, dweller, husbandman, farmer, countryman, derived from the verb root *bu*, to dwell ('neighbour' is literally 'nigh-dweller'). 'Boor', like its synonym 'peasant', soon took on the derogatory sense it still has: in 1598 John Florio wrote of 'a lubber, a clowne, a boore, a rude fellow'. 'Villain', from Old French *vilein* (derived in turn from the Latin *villa*, a farm) has had two senses from the beginning of the 1300s: 'peasant occupier entirely subject to

a lord' and 'a man of ignoble ideas and instincts'. Do we owe the derogatory sense of words denoting land-workers to the Normans?

No such connotations attach to 'bor', meaning neighbour or gossip, the East Anglian variant of 'boor'. I first met the word as a £5-a-week reporter with the *Eastern Daily Press* in Norwich. Occasionally I had to report on official dinners, say of a local trade association. The best thing was the statutory comedian, especially if he talked Norfolk, which I still think the best-humoured, richest dialect in the kingdom; 'bor' occurred in practically every other sentence.

From pure pleasure to pure sadness. *Boer*, farmer, is the exact Dutch equivalent of 'boor' in its original, non-derogatory sense (cf. German *Bauer*), but I never hear the English word 'Boer' without feeling sorrow and fear for the people of South Africa and the fraught situation they have inherited from history.

30 JUNE 1985

B OSPORUS. Mr Douglas Kershaw, of Beadlam, Yorkshire, asks if it should have an 'h'. Atlases have 'p' only. Dictionaries are permissive. The Oxford Dictionary for Writers and Editors is firm: '*not* Bosph-'. A classical scholar agrees. 'The Greek *bos*', he said, 'means "ox" or "heifer", *poros* means "ford".' Like Oxford? 'Exactly.' In this context *bos* means 'heifer'. The Bosporus, according to legend, was crossed by Io, one of Zeus's many beloveds, after he had changed her into a heifer to help her escape from his enraged wife Hera (some say it was the work of Hera herself).

21 APRIL 1985

St Austell, Cornwall

DEAR MR SILVERLIGHT, *Who on earth is your 'classical scholar'? The great Liddell and great Scott would certainly not agree with him that 'the Greek* bos *means "ox" or "heifer": there is no such word in Greek as* bos, *which is Latin. The Greek form is* bous, *which survives in our word 'boustrophedon'.*

Yours sincerely

DAVID PUGH

The mistake had several causes, including my misreading of my abridged Liddell and Scott's Greek lexicon, and had nothing to do with my classical scholar who, when he saw the piece in print, told me that the word should indeed have been *bous*. However, he went on, 'the Greek name of the strait is Bosporus, not Bousporus; and according to Liddell and Scott, this is "a solitary instance" of *bos*, in composition, for *bous*'.

Mr Pugh tempered his reproof with kind words about the column in general; I was even more comforted by his introducing me to the delightful word 'boustrophedon'. The Greek word from which it is transliterated comes from *bous* and *strophe*, a turning (cf. 'catastrophe', the original meaning of which was 'turning point of a play'). My lexicon translates it 'Turning like oxen in ploughing' and goes on: 'of the early manner of Greek writing which went from left to right, and right to left alternately [or, as the OED has it, 'like the course of a plough in successive furrows']. So Solon's laws were written.' The earliest example of the word in English is dated 1783.

The famous Law Code of Gortyna, in Crete, is written boustrophedon. 'Carved on stone blocks,' John Bowman writes in his *Travellers' Guide to Crete*, 'it stands upright as it stood when the Romans came and incorporated it into their Odeon . . . More than 17 000 characters are carved in the stones. The language is an archaic Doric dialect of Greek, and most of its eighteen letters are recognisably Greek . . . The laws deal essentially with civil matters such as marriage, divorce, adultery, property rights, adoption, inheritance and mortgage of property'.

B RITAIN. Lord Colyton (who, then Mr Henry Hopkinson, was Minister of State for Colonial Affairs 1952–56) wrote to *The Times* in August urging that we 'get away from the perpetual "UK" and get back to "GB"'. Mr Gershon Ellenbogen wrote in reply: 'Great Britain consists of England, with Wales, and Scotland (Act of Union with Scotland, 1706): the United

Kingdom is Great Britain and Northern Ireland (Act of Union with Ireland, 1800: Government of Ireland Act, 1920): and the United Kingdom is the State for the purpose of international relations.'

I don't like 'UK' either, but then I don't like initials – having spent most of my childhood there, the United States is a second country to me, but I never see 'US' without remembering that, in the army, that is how faulty equipment was shown in the quartermaster's books, i.e. unserviceable. My main dislike is the term 'Britain'. There was Ancient Britain and Roman Britain (Cymbeline was King of Britain). There was the Battle of Britain and the Festival of Britain. 'Britain' exists only in association with something else. However, in Letters Patent creating peers and appointing certain officers of state to high position, such as the Clerks of the House of Lords and House of Commons, Elizabeth II is described as, 'by the Grace of God', Queen 'of the United Kingdom of Great Britain *and Northern Ireland*' (my italics). To omit the italicised words when speaking or writing of the country we live in today is a grave slight to the inhabitants of the province.

Britain, of course, is even more 'wrong', but that is a lost cause. I dodge the problem by using 'this country' – I also like to speak of 'the kingdom' as in, say, 'the best beer in the kingdom'. For headlines, UK will do.

13 OCTOBER 1985

BUREAU. A word much in the news recently.* I am puzzled by the way it is pronounced by the BBC (and by the Home Secretary, Mr Leon Brittan), with the emphasis, as often as not, on the second syllable. That pronunciation is shown first in the OED, with '*bu*reau' as an alternative, but the entry was prepared for publication in 1888. Nowadays the Concise Oxford has it the other way round, as does Chambers. Webster's Collegiate, the Longman Dictionary of Contemporary English (which is aimed primarily at foreign rather than native speakers of English) and Collins do not show 'bur*eau*' at all. Professor A. C. Gimson (see AUTHORITY), editor of the Everyman English Pronouncing Dictionary, reckons that more than two-thirds of the population say '*bu*reau'.

6 MAY 1984

* On 17 April 1984, during a demonstration outside the Libyan People's Bureau (formerly the Libyan Embassy) in St James's Square, WPC Yvonne Fletcher was shot dead by someone inside the building. A siege was mounted, diplomatic relations were broken off and the Libyan representatives were given until 29 April to leave the country. They left on the 27th.

Chigwell, Essex

DEAR MR SILVERLIGHT, *I wonder if you know of 'the broo'? Unemployed Scots are 'on the broo' or go to draw the 'broo money'. What began as the Labour Exchanges in the Lloyd George era were later transmuted into Unemployment Bureau. In Glasgow this became* buroo *and then 'broo'. It is still in use.*

Best wishes

ALAN SMITH
(co-author of the Papermac To Coin a Phrase)

BUSKING: a word of many meanings and uncertain derivation. So I learnt on looking it up after hearing a busker perform – most elegantly – when I was changing tube trains in London.

First a fashion note. The noun 'busk' is defined in the 1934 Concise Oxford: 'Rigid strip stiffening corset-front'. It derives from the French *busc*, 'Busk (of stays)' – Cassell's French–English dictionary, 1938. The new Concise doesn't have 'busk'; Collins–Robert (1978) doesn't have *busc*. Back to usage. The Oxford English Dictionary has two main sections on the verb 'busk'. One, 'obsolete except Scotch and northern dialect', is '*generally thought*' (my italics) to derive from Old Norse *bua*, 'to prepare', and includes the senses 'to dress' and 'to get ready'. The other is introduced as 'nautical' and '*apparently*' (my italics) derives from obsolete French *busquer*, 'to shift, filch; prowle, catch by hook or crook; *busquer fortune*, to go seek his fortune' – A Dictionarie of the French and English Tongues, by Randle Cotgrave, 1611.

17

In this second section are: '1. To tack . . . to cruise as a pirate . . . 2. To go about seeking for . . . 3. Slang. See quotations. (But perhaps this is a distinct word . . .)'. One quotation, dated 1851, reads: 'Busking is going into public houses and playing and singing and dancing' – Henry Mayhew's *London Labour and the London Poor. Busquer* is the source given in the Concise Oxford ('perhaps') and the Longman English Language ('probably'); Chambers says it is 'probably' the Spanish *buscar*; Collins and Webster say the origin is unknown.

So to that busker at Leicester Square Station. It was rush hour, I was tired and bad-tempered. Then, gradually, I became aware of a diversion: a young man, neatly dressed, kempt, was playing some baroque composition on an amplified mandolin and playing it well; it made a lovely noise. I contributed 20 pence and walked on, refreshed – to be confronted by a poster that read: 'WARNING. Buskers and street musicians are not allowed to perform on London Transport property. Offenders will be prosecuted. Maximum penalty £50.' The authorities, I gather, do not hunt down buskers over-zealously, although actions are brought occasionally.

9 FEBRUARY 1986

C=APPING. Writing about the Rates Bill last month I suggested that the expression 'rate-capping' (see entry) derived from the oil industry, as in capping a well. The earliest example I found was in a *Times* report of 2 August last year. Last week I received a cutting from the *National Student*, the journal of the National Union of Students, in which the word 'capping' in relation to public funds had been used more than three years earlier. Formerly local education authorities used to contribute to a 'pool' of money for higher education, out of which non-university colleges, a polytechnic, say, could finance new buildings, teacher training courses etc.; its LEA in effect shared the cost with the other 103 authorities whether they liked it or not; the system was open-ended or, as they say now, 'demand-led'. Then, in 1979, the Council of Local Education Authorities asked the Government for new regulations to 'cap the pool'. This, apparently, was the first time 'capping' had been used in that sense, and must surely be the origin of 'rate-capping'.

Mr Peter Sloman, formerly Education Officer of the Metropolitan Authorities, writing in the *National Student*'s March 1980 issue, explained that under the new regulations a 'quantum' (in the old sense of agreed amount, not 'quantum jump') was shared among LEAs 'on a formula reflecting the amount of advanced work in each area'. His article began: '"Capping the pool", a metaphor drawn from oil technology, suggests highly expert engineers struggling desperately to fit a cap on top of a pipe connected to a gas- or oilfield forcing up material under immense pressure.' (My colleague Christine Moir, of *The Observer*'s Business section, tells me that when steel furnaces used to overflow, before modern methods of temperature control came in, they were 'capped' with 'plugs' of wet clay.)

An article in the *New Statesman* last month on Common Market wrangles and attempts to limit milk production was headlined DAIRY FARMERS CAPPED. The villain of the piece was the Common Agricultural Policy, CAP.

15 APRIL 1984

CELSIUS/CENTIGRADE.

Very quietly, a small but interesting change has been made in one of our more sacred institutions: weather reports. The Meteorological Office has decided that the term Celsius shall be used for temperatures instead of Centigrade. (Some of us, nearly 20 years after it came in, haven't really come to terms with Centigrade yet, but let that pass; Fahrenheit equivalents will continue to be given.)

When asking its staff last month to encourage the use of Celsius 'as widely as possible', the office said the change had already taken place 'in most countries'. The order didn't say so, but this is in keeping with the trend in science to name units of measurement after their inventors. At one time electromagnetic wave frequencies were given in 'cycles per second'. The generally accepted term now is Hertz, after Heinrich Hertz, the German physicist who invented the measurement: long and medium wave frequencies, for example, are given in kilohertz, kHz, short wave in megahertz, mHz. Anders Celsius, the Swedish astronomer who invented the Centigrade thermometer, has had to wait longer for general recognition – he died, aged 42, in 1744; Hertz, at 36, in 1894. One Hertz is one cycle per second; the Celsius scale, 0 to 100 degrees, is the Centigrade

19

scale; the changes are of term only, not measurement.

On BBC Television and ITV the London Weather Centre forecasters give both Celsius and Fahrenheit. On Radio 3 and Radio 4 they say: 'Temperatures will vary from 5 to 8 degrees' (or whatever, not specifying a scale), '41 to 46 degrees Fahrenheit'. A forecaster told me the BBC had asked him not to use Celsius on Radio 4; it would be all right on Radio 3. There seem to have been second thoughts about the adaptability of Radio 3 audiences too.

10 MARCH 1985

Banbury, Oxon.

DEAR MR SILVERLIGHT, *You might be interested to know that there is a more fundamental temperature scale in which the units are the same size as the Celsius degree, but which has its origin at −273° (approx.) C and is based on the thermodynamics of an ideal gas. This scale used to be known as the Absolute Scale of Temperature, but is now known as the Kelvin Scale, and temperatures are stated as so many Kelvin. The temperature at which water boils under normal atmospheric pressure, is, for example, 373 K (NB not degrees K, just K). This scale, and its unit, are named after William Thomson, who took the title Lord Kelvin. It was he who established that the properties of gases could be made the basis of an absolute scale of temperature.*

Yours sincerely

M. S. RUDDOCK

One of many letters amplifying, modifying and correcting me on Celsius/Centigrade – no more than I deserved for rashly venturing out of my depth in scientific matters; most of the letters were friendly. Comments included the following (my original observations in italics).

'The Celsius scale is the Centigrade scale.' Mr Mick Nott, a physicist, of Orton Longueville, Peterborough, wrote that a temperature scale is defined by fixed points. Celsius's are the melting point of pure ice and the temperature of steam, 0° and 100° respectively. 'A centigrade [note the lower case 'c'] scale just means that the interval between any arbitrary two fixed points is divided into 100 equal divisions. So the Celsius scale is a centigrade scale, but a centigrade scale is not necessarily

the Celsius scale.' Others pointed out that adopting the term 'Celsius' avoids still another ambiguity. The OED's first definition of 'grade' (the entry was prepared for publication in 1900) is 'a degree of angular measurement . . . the 90th part of a right angle. . . . In the centesimal mode . . . the hundredth part of a right angle'. So, although it does not appear in that sense in the OED, 'centigrade' also means a 10 000th part of a right angle. A pretty small angle, to be sure, but it is in print – in the HMSO pamphlet 'Changing to the Metric System', first published in 1965. Mr Ruddock too wrote in his letter of 'the practice of describing the division of the right-angle into 100 parts as Centigrade', and added: 'indeed it is possible to buy electronic calculators which will operate using this 100-part division as well as the more familiar 90 degrees or the mathematically convenient radian measure.'

'The trend in science is to name units of measurement after their inventors.' Dr C. J. W. Hooper, of Stevenage in Hertfordshire, wrote that the trend has been going on for many decades, for example: 'ampere' (1881), 'faraday' (1904), 'watt' (1882). Against this T. A. Willetts, of Kelsall in Cheshire, wrote that while it is correct to say that the trend to name units after their inventors is an old one, there has also been a recent event: the decision not only to rename old, impersonally named units after scientists (e.g. Centigrade) but also so to name new units, such as the 'newton' (unit of force) and the 'pascal' (unit of pressure).

This event was the coming into existence of SI, the International System of Units – the more commonly used abbreviation is from the name in French, *Système International d'Unités*. It was derived, says the *Encyclopaedia Britannica*, 'from the metric system of physical units and adopted, defined and named in 1954–60 by the General Conference on Weights and Measures (an international controlling body) as the system of choice for general world-wide use. The six basic units in the SI system are the metre, kilogram, second, ampere, degree Kelvin and candela – for length, mass, time, electric current, tempera-ture and luminous intensity. Other units are derived from them.' 'So', Mr Willetts wrote, 'you were right first time – except that it was a sudden change rather than a trend.'

'Heinrich Hertz invented the measurement for electromagnetic wave frequencies.' Readers said that that was most unlikely. According to *Britannica*, he *was* the first to broadcast and receive radio waves. Most complaints were about another mistake in the bit

about Hertz: my giving the abbreviation of megahertz, million hertz, as 'mHz'. It should have been 'MHz'; 'mHz' would represent 'millihertz', the very low frequency of one wave per thousand seconds. On this Mr Willetts extended his sympathy: 'After years of trying to get non-tech typists to accept that MHz and mHz differ, I think that this is the worst feature of SI. And if you are stuck with block capitals, as in a telex, you are in real trouble.'

A note on broadcast weather forecasts. I am pleased to report both that Radio 3 and 4 decided that their audiences could be exposed to Celsius and that they have retained Fahrenheit too. As Fritz Spiegl wrote in the *Listener* of 6 February 1986, 'my body knows when it has a temperature of 99° and needs a couple of aspirins, while 37° means nothing. In summer I can tell the difference between 78° and 80°F, but centigrade, with its larger units, doesn't give any such idea. Which is why the headlines will never scream at us "41°! PHEW WHAT A SCORCHER".'

CHARM is not a quality I prize. It smacks of the meretricious, and I dislike hearing the word applied to someone I respect (not that I would like to hear such a person, or myself for that matter, described as 'charmless'). Edmund Burke said of a slogan coined by a political opponent: 'Of this stamp is the cant of *Not men, but measures*; a sort of charm by which many people get loose from honourable engagement.' Albert Camus said: 'You know what charm is: a way of getting the answer yes without having asked any clear question.' In Alan Jay Lerner's *My Fair Lady* Rex Harrison sings, 'Oozing charm from every pore,/He oiled his way around the floor'. When Tom Jones, Deputy Secretary to the Cabinet in the Great War, said Lloyd George 'could charm a bird off a branch' he wasn't paying L. G. a compliment. (Clemenceau, according to an anecdote told me by Dr Conor Cruise O'Brien, took a different, very French view. After one of the many rows during the Versailles Treaty negotiations, an aide he was talking to said of Lloyd George, '*C'est un con.*' Clemenceau replied, '*Non, il n'en a ni le charme ni la profondeur.*') Consider the irritating 1970s usage as quoted in the 1984 edition of Partridge: 'She screams across the pub at him, "You're nothing but a big, fat, idle swine!" Interested listener, encouragingly, "Charming!"'

The word comes from Latin *carmen*, song, but also 'a magic formula, an incantation' (Lewis and Short) – '*Carminibus Circe socios mutavit Ulixi*': With spells Circe changed the comrades of Ulysses (Vergil) – and it retained the sense of occult influence in English. In time 'charm' and its derivatives distanced themselves from such associations. The OED defines 'charming' as: '1. Using charms; exercising magic power. 2. Fascinating, highly pleasing or delightful to the senses. (At first distinctly from 1, but now [1889] used without any thought of that, and as a milder form of "enchanting".)'

'Enchanting'. Illogically, I find that word pleasing. I can think of no higher compliment.

10 AUGUST 1986

CHIC. Recently Roger Boyes wrote in *The Times* of 'the Warsaw chiceria', the Polish new rich who are making fortunes out of such activities as private trading in cars and other scarce goods and 'exploiting the more profitable branches of private agriculture'. On the telephone Mr Boyes told me he got the word from the German *Schickeria*, a set of people noted for their elegance, café society, or, as Miss Mechthild Offermans at the Goethe Institute in London says, 'high snobiety'; the stress of *Schickeria* is on the second 'i' – which indicates the pronunciation of 'chiceria' – and it is derived from the similarly-pronounced Italian *sciccheria*, which also means smart set and, as can be guessed, comes from the French *chic*. Of course, but where does *chic* come from? 'Of doubtful origin', says the big French dictionary *Robert*, 'perhaps from the German *Schick*', a sixteenth-century word meaning aptitude.

All very interesting. Even more interesting to me is the ambiguity of *chic* – your truly well-bred French man or woman would not like to be described as *chic*. *Littré*, the most authoritative traditional French dictionary, agrees with *Robert* about its probable German derivation in its usual sense. However, *Littré* also gives an earlier sense of artifice, slyness, specious subtleties: 'This man understands *le chic*, he is well versed in the tricks of *la chicane*' (which means legal quibbling; our word 'chicanery' is derived from it). One of the senses of 'chic' in Webster is modish. In the sixties we had 'Radical Chic', Tom Wolfe's account of a party given by Leonard

23

Bernstein in New York for the Black Panthers. Now Roger Boyes extends the sense of smart set to describe people who are little better than black marketeers. Altogether it is a classic case of pejoration, the process by which the meaning of a word is worsened. (The opposite process, just as fascinating and mysterious, by which the meaning of a word is improved, is known as amelioration.)

3 JUNE 1984

CHRISTMAS, I am reminded by the *Everyman's Dictionary of First Names*, by Leslie Dunkling and William Gosling (Dent), was used as a Christian name throughout the nineteenth century for someone born on that day. However, it goes on, 'seasonal births now tend to be marked by such names as "Natalie", "Natasha", "Noel" and "Noelle"'. Similarly, 'Easter' has been replaced by the French 'Pascal' and 'Pascale'. I say I am 'reminded' of all this since I first learnt it from the *Oxford Dictionary of English Christian Names*, by E. G. Withycombe (handsomely acknowledged by the Everyman authors). What neither book explains is why other festivals have not become Christian names too. What's wrong with Epiphany, or Trinity, or Whitsun – better still in its Greek derivation, Pentecost? (Miss Withycombe says 'Pentecost', in use till the seventeenth century, survives as 'Pascoe' in Cornwall. None of those names seems as outlandish as many of the Everyman names. Indeed, I get a strong impression from the book of the irresponsibility, if not downright cruelty, of some parents towards their children. Take 'Pearline' – how do you pronounce it, *peerline*? *pairline*? (It's a development of 'Pearl'.) Or 'Pixie' – how winsome can you get? (Inevitably 'Winsome' appears too.) And what about 'Zeppelina', 'a name given to one or two English girls during the First World War'?

The Everyman is more comprehensive than the Oxford: '4000 entries,' says the blurb, 'mentioning over 10 000 names', against nearly 1400 main entries. The contrast sounds overwhelming, but many of the Everyman entries are pet names (e.g. 'Jim') and many of the 10 000 names simple spelling variations. Certainly I shan't desert Miss Withycombe, who, with only one broad column on the page – the Everyman has two, like other dictionaries – is easier to read and thus to

24

browse in. I have other reservations. 'Clemency', says Everyman, 'appears to be totally obsolete.' I know of four girls called Clemency, besides Betjeman's 'Clemency the General's daughter'. In the entry for 'Tetty', pet form of 'Elizabeth', there is no mention of surely the most famous Tetty of all, Dr Johnson's wife. Again, '"Charmian" *should* [my italics] be pronounced *Karmian*.' It comes from the Greek *charma*, joy, with the 'ch' pronounced as in 'loch', but I have never, in all the times I've seen *Cleopatra*, heard it pronounced that way. Miss Withycombe says, less didactically but more correctly, 'The correct pronunciation would be *karmean*.'

These are niggles. Messrs Dunkling and Gosling are authoritative, thorough and interesting. Both books are musts, and not just for prospective parents.

23 DECEMBER 1984

Mr Philip McEvansoneya, of Barnstaple in Devon, wrote: 'What about the sadly ignored seventeenth-century sculptor Epiphanius Evesham (1570– after 1633)?' According to 'Sculpture in Britain 1530–1830' by Margaret Whinney, in the *Penguin History of Art*, he was 'the first English-born sculptor of any personality. . . . His works have a refinement, and what is more a depth of feeling that is rare in his age. Evesham, the fourteenth son of a Herefordshire squire, received his unusual name because he was born on the feast of the Epiphany.' A few days later Mr McEvansoneya, quoting the book *Hilliard and Oliver* by Mary Edmond, wrote: 'I have just come across Epiphane Oliver, the mother of the miniaturist Isaac Oliver (1556?–1617).' Oliver was a pupil of Hilliard and, according to the *Dictionary of National Biography*, 'often excelled him'. (Asked about his own unusual name, Mr McEvansoneya said it was believed to be a corruption of the Cornish name Swavenney. 'Other explanations have seemed rather far-fetched – it is one of the 101 things I shall look into when I have time.')

Listed among contemporaries of Epiphanius Evesham in the *Penguin History* was a family of Dutch emigrants, Gerard, John and Matthias Christmas. And Dr Bernard Freedman, who contributes an 'occasional mini-column in the *British Medical Journal*' dealing with medical terminology, wrote: 'Eponymous diseases are almost without exception named after the doctor(s) who first described them in medical literature [e.g. Parkinson's disease].' An exception is Christmas Disease, 'a variant of

25

haemophilia, named after S. Christmas, the first patient to have his condition reported'.

H. B. Collier, of Edmonton, Alberta, wrote: 'I once knew a Miss Rhoda Palfrey. Perhaps her parents did not know the meaning of "palfrey" and maybe they were trying to be funny.'

COINS.

'Sorry about these', apologised the greengrocer, giving me four £1 coins as change from a £5 note. You hear jokes: why are £1 coins called 'maggies' (or 'scargills', depending on the joker's political sympathies)? *Daily Mail* leading articles have denounced them. Why all this hostility? I like them: their durability, what with the increasing scruffiness of £1 notes; the elegance of their design; the inscriptions round the edge.

The first, the £1 coin of Great Britain (as it is known to the staff of the Mint), with the Royal Arms on the reverse, was issued in April 1983; with the inscription *Decus et tutamen*, a phrase from Vergil, which is translated as 'an ornament and a safeguard'; the ornament is the lettering, but this is also a safeguard against forgery. The Scots variant appeared in the following April and the Welsh variant this year. Superficially they are all very alike (which is why, unobservantly, I have only recently become aware of the later coins) but the differences are interesting. The reverse of the Scots coin is a beautiful, slightly stylised thistle; the inscription is *Nemo me impune lacessit*, motto of the Order of the Thistle and of three Scots regiments: the Scots Guards, the Royal Scots and the Black Watch. It means 'No one provokes me with impunity' and no one, so says the Secretary of the Order, Mr Malcolm Innes of Edingight (who is also Lord Lyon, King of Arms), knows its origin: it is lost in antiquity. The reverse of the Welsh coin has a leek, also beautiful and slightly stylised. The inscription, *Pleidiol wyf i'm gwlad*, 'True am I to my country', comes from the Welsh national anthem, 'Land of My Fathers'. Next year the variant of Northern Ireland will be struck, with a flax plant on the reverse, and that of England in 1987, with an oak; both will have the inscription *Decus et tutamen*. It is all a splendidly imaginative concept, and one the whole of Great Britain can be proud of.

14 JULY 1985

COMPLEX/COMPLICATED.

In a discussion last week on the miners' strike I heard the situation in the Durham coalfield described as 'complex'. I had an idea that the speaker meant 'complicated', but I wasn't clear about the distinction between the two words. Dictionaries are not all that helpful on the whole – Chambers makes things more difficult by defining the verb 'complicate' as 'to twist or plait together'. This echoes the derivation of 'complex', which derives from Latin *com-* and *plectere*, to braid; 'complicate' comes from *complicare*, to fold together. An exception is Webster's Collegiate which, in a useful note, says: '"Complex" suggests the unavoidable result of a necessary combining and does not imply a fault or failure; "complicated" applies to what offers great difficulty in understanding, solving or explaining.' One computer can be more complex than another. The situation in the Durham coalfield is complicated.

Another pair of frequently confused 'lookalike' words is 'turbid' and 'turgid'. *The Observer* has been taken to task for writing about the *Political Quarterly*'s 'turgid waters' when, so writes Mr John Wood of Reading, it meant 'turbid'. 'Turgid' (from *turgere*, to swell), he says, 'describes pompous, overblown prose (rather like this letter)'. 'Turbid' (from *turba*, a crowd) means muddy, opaque. 'Both words', he adds, 'may apply to writing, but "turgid" may surely never be used to describe water.' Mr Wood is quite right. The distinction between this second pair of words, unlike the first pair, is blessedly uncomplicated. (See DEPRECIATE/DEPRECATE and LINCH/LYNCH.)

7 OCTOBER 1984

CORDUROY.

'A strong durable fabric with a rounded cord . . . surface formed by a cut pile yarn. . . . Its name is probably derived from the French *corde du roi*' – *Britannica*. Unfortunately, 'no such name has ever been used in French', says a note in the OED. 'Corduroy' is 'apparently of English invention: either originally intended, or soon after assumed, to represent a supposed Fr. *corde du roi*.' (I can confirm that the expression *corde du roi* does not appear in the seven-volume *Grand Larousse de la Langue Française*.) The OED note quotes a French source as enumerating among a list of articles

27

manufactured at Sens in 1807 *'étoffes de coton futaine* [fustian], *kings-cordes,* evidently from English'. (I wonder how the French pronounced *kings-cordes?)*

Dr John Hibbs of Birmingham, a consultant in transport, quoting from *The History of Roads: from Amber Route to Motorway* by Heinrich Schreiber (Barrie and Rockcliffe, 1961), writes in a letter that 'ancient European highways, such as the prehistoric amber roads, were laid across soft ground by placing logs at right angles to the direction of the traffic and that these were "corduroy roads"'. Dr Hibbs adds that such roads, which date back to the fifth century BC, 'would be a series of alternate ups and downs, much like those in the cloth'. Is there a connection? Possibly, but the dates of examples indicate that it was the cloth that suggested the name for the roads. The earliest example of the cloth sense is dated 1787, of the road sense 1822.

The expression 'corduroy roads' originated in the United States and by all accounts they were hideously uncomfortable to travel on. An example dated 1830 reads, 'The anguish we suffered from the corduroy crossways' – from *Lawrie Todd, or the Settlers in the Woods,* by John Galt. Gore Vidal, in his *Lincoln,* describes Lincoln's wife Mary going to an army review in an ambulance along a corduroy road 'set across a sea of red Virginia mud and swampland. Mary had never in her life known such discomfort.' At one point, 'on a section of corduroy road made up of trees of different sizes', the ambulance 'sprang into the air. The two ladies, as one, left their seat and would have departed the ambulance entirely had the back section not been roofed in. As it was, two large, splendidly decorated hats prevented the heads from breaking open but at the cost of two miraculous examples of the milliner's craft, now crushed.'

19 MAY 1985

When working on the derivation of 'corduroy' I went straight to the big Oxford, bypassing modern dictionaries. That was an error of judgment. No fresh information has been produced since 1893 – when the 'corduroy' entry went to press – but the conclusions of later etymologists are worth reporting. The key word is 'duroy': 'coarse woollen fabric manufactured in Somersetshire in the 18th century', says the OED, adding, however, that 'it has no apparent connection with "corduroy"'. That is why I did not mention it in the piece. However, according to the Oxford Dictionary of English Etymology (1966), 'corduroy' probably comes from 'cord' (the plural 'cords', it says, 'is applied to a ribbed fabric in Wolstenholme's Patent 1776') plus the obsolete '"duroy" . . . coarse West of England woollen stuff, of unknown origin'. The 1976 Concise Oxford, as Miss C. M. Lovett, of Barnstaple in Devon, points out in a letter, has a shortened version of that derivation. So, with slight variations, does the Reader's Digest Great Illustrated, and – except that it says 'perhaps' instead of 'probably' – the Longman Dictionary of the English Language.

The Etymological Dictionary rejects two other suggested origins of 'corduroy'. One is 'colour-de-roy', 'king's colour' or purple. This, says Mr Brian O'Kill of Longman, was the source preferred by the Nottingham University academic Ernest Weekley (whose German-born wife Frieda ran away with D. H. Lawrence). The other is the surname 'Corderoy', which the OED gives as a possible source. Etymologists are wary of proper names as origins, Mr O'Kill says. Under 'blanket' (from French *blanc* and *-ette*) the OED has: 'The Thomas Blanket, to whom gossip attributes the origin of the name, if he really existed, doubtless took his name from the article.' And under 'tank', meaning 'a form of armoured car having caterpillar (tractor) wheels, first put into commission on 15 Sept. 1916', the 1933 Supplement to the OED has the note: 'The claim that the name was adopted from that of Thomas Tank Burall, a tractor designer, has no basis in fact.'

Readers who have lived on the Continent write that in several languages the word for 'corduroy' is *Manchester*. That is entirely appropriate in view of the importance of Manchester in textiles, but it seems that the usage is declining. In Germany, for instance, the increasingly universal *cords* has replaced it for people born since World War Two. It still applies, I am told, in Czechoslovakia (*manšestr – š=sh*) and the Swiss canton of Valais (*le manchester*).

7 JULY 1985

COUNT NOUNS. Mrs E. L. Gray, of King's Langley, in Hertfordshire, asks for 'help in resolving a deep division in my

family when playing Scrabble as to whether such words as "oxygen", "ozone" etc. can have "s" added to them. My son maintains that as there can only be one of them, they cannot be pluralised. When it is pointed out that "two beers" or "two teas" are common usage, he says, "That's different!"'

At first I could not think where to start looking for an answer. Then, days later, up from the subconscious swam the word 'countable' and, with it, the idea of looking it up in the Longman Dictionary of Contemporary English (*Eldoce* from here on). I was right: 'A countable noun can also be called a count noun . . . opposite, uncountable' (some dictionaries, I find, have 'mass' for 'uncountable'). A 'count noun' is one that 'has a plural and that can be used with . . . "a" or "an". In this dictionary, count nouns are often marked "C".' (I had previously noted a 'C' in entries and 'U', uncountable, but had never hoisted them in; I suspect I wasn't alone in this.) 'Oxygen' in *Eldoce* is uncompromisingly marked 'U', so it cannot have a plural or be used with 'an'. However, ten entries down the page is 'ozone', also 'U', and defined: 'air that is pleasant to breathe, esp. near the sea . . . 2. *a type* of oxygen' (my italics). Why then can't 'oxygen' be plural? And why not 'ozones' – might not the ozone of, say, Southend differ from that of, say, Brighton? Logically, perhaps, but usage notoriously defies logic. A scientist tells me: 'You *could* say "oxygens", but you wouldn't.' 'Beer', 'tea' etc. are 'U' in *Eldoce* when meaning the drink, 'C' when meaning 'glasses of', 'cups of' etc.

22 JUNE 1986

My scientist friend agreed – too late, unfortunately, to correct that piece – that he had been slightly misleading in telling me that one would not say 'oxygens'. In fact, I was on to something, even if misguidedly. Mr John Lamper, of Shillingstone in Dorset, wrote: 'Common usage suggests that such plurals are possible, and as a chemistry teacher, I find myself using them every working day. In discussing atoms of various elements within a molecule, my students and I would talk about the number of oxygens, chlorines etc. These plurals are really verbal shorthand for "oxygen atoms", "chlorine atoms" and so on. I would happily accept such plurals in a game of Scrabble, but would expect my opponent to justify them in scientific terms.'

Mr Tom Fay, CChem, FRSC (Chartered Chemist, Fellow of

the Royal Society of Chemistry) of Manchester wrote that he and his fellow chemists had been regularly using the word 'oxygens' and others like it 'for the whole of my more than forty years' involvement with chemistry. Indeed, the usage goes back as far as Dalton (1803) or 1811, when the Swedish chemist Jöns Jakob Berzelious proposed the present chemical notation system. They are used in describing the composition of chemical compounds. Ordinary table sugar (sucrose) has the formula $C_{12}H_{22}O_{11}$, and would be said by a chemist to contain twelve carbons, twenty-two hydrogens and eleven oxygens. The case of "ozone" is slightly different in that there is only one ozone, O_3, triatomic oxygen, containing "three oxygens" [ordinary oxygen is diatomic, "two oxygens"]. Thus in strict chemical terms the ozone of Southend will not differ from that of Brighton (or of Blackpool or of Scarborough!). If, however, the word "ozone" is defined as a property of seaside air, then there may indeed be several "ozones".'

Mr T. R. Pearce of Middlesbrough, commenting on my explanation that 'beer' and 'tea' when meaning the drink were 'uncountable' and so could not be used in the plural, but were 'countable' when meaning 'glasses of' and 'cups of', wrote robustly, though in a friendly manner, 'Rubbish – any beer drinker would confirm it, there are many beers, just as there are many wines. Every brewer produces more than one, often half a dozen or more. And would you not say that China tea, Ceylon tea and Indian tea are different teas? Never mind "types of" – the plural will do well enough.'

13 JULY 1986

CRAFT. Recently I was involved in a correspondence in the *Listener* about the verb 'to craft'. One of the letters asked why it appeared in the 12-volume Oxford English Dictionary and in the Concise Oxford and not in the two-volume Shorter Oxford, which the writer 'habitually relied on'. The answer needs a bit of spelling out. The OED definition, 'to make or devise skilfully', was prepared for publication in 1893, with an example dated *c*.1420: 'Have a cisterne . . . Let crafte it up pleasaunt as it may suffice.' The Shorter, an abridgement of the OED not basically altered since it came out in 1933 (a revised edition is expected to appear in the 1990s), did not carry 'to craft', possibly to save space; in any case the OED had labelled it 'obs.' and 'rare'. The 1933 Concise did not have it either, but the drastically revised 1976 edition did, with the definition: '*make in skilled manner' (the asterisk denotes 'chiefly US'). The point is that the revisers of the 1976 edition were able to draw on Volume I of A Supplement to the OED, which appeared in 1972 and showed the verb as 'revived, esp. in the US'. The first example was: 'Performances such as *Lycidas* were essentially public events, monuments crafted out of a shared language' (*Listener*, 14 February 1963).

At first I felt surprise that all this was not general knowledge. Then I remembered that not so long ago I didn't know it either. Well after this column became a regular feature in *The Observer* I discovered that no OED entry was later than 1928, when the dictionary was completed; the first instalment (A–Ant) went to press in 1884 (one of the compositors was working at the dictionary throughout the whole period). This basic piece of information should not have been much of a shock – I had been using the dictionary since the forties – but it was, and I went on exploring. Besides rudimentary facts such as the dates mentioned above, when the various Oxford dictionaries were published, I learnt how members of the Philological Society had launched the project of the OED (at first called the New English Dictionary) in 1858 and had begun to recruit what became 'an army of volunteers' (Preface to the OED), many of them parsons and schoolteachers – and their families – in order to collect quotations from Chaucer (and earlier), Shakespeare, Jerome K. Jerome etc., etc., etc., illustrating the changes in the sense of words over the centuries. And I learnt how that master of lexicography, James Murray, the first editor, began work in 1878 organising the vast, infinitely daunting mass of material into what is the definitive history of the English language. By his death, in 1915, he had three co-editors working with him, but he had edited more than half the dictionary himself. His granddaughter Kathleen Murray tells the story beautifully in her biography of him, *Caught in a Web of Words* (Yale University Press).

23 SEPTEMBER 1984

32

DEACONESS.

I have always had doubts about the suffix '-ess'. At best it is unnecessary – a woman GP or heart specialist is not a 'doctress' – at worst, as in 'poetess', it is derogatory (and even then it is unnecessary: if one wished to make the point that the lady is an inferior poet, there is the much better put-down 'poetaster').

However, the debate in the General Synod of the Church of England about the ordination of women suggests one case in which I think the suffix *is* necessary. At the heart of the matter are words, the Words of Institution in the Communion Service, with which the priest consecrates the bread and wine: ' . . . grant that we receiving these thy creatures of bread and wine, according to thy Son our Saviour Jesus Christ's holy institution . . . who, in the same night that he was betrayed, took Bread; and, when he had given thanks, he brake it, and gave it to his disciples, saying, Take, eat, this is my Body which is given for you . . . Likewise after supper he took the Cup; and when he had given thanks, he gave it to them, saying, Drink ye all of this; for this is my Blood of the New Testament, which is shed for you and for many for the remission of sins . . . '

A deaconess cannot say those words. Again, in the Absolution the priest asks God to 'Have mercy upon you; pardon and deliver you from all your sins'. A deaconess cannot say 'you'; it has to be 'us'. A technicality? For a congregation at Communion, perhaps. But take a patient dying in hospital who wants to be given specifically personal absolution. If the chaplain is a deaconess she cannot pronounce it. Of course a deacon too is not allowed to say the Words of Institution or to give personal absolution, but he is on a 12-month probation. If he keeps his nose clean he will become a priest. Unless the law is changed a deaconess will never be one.

In 'authoress,' 'poetess' etc., the suffix, although a solecism, does not indicate discrimination. In 'deaconess' it does, which is why I describe it as necessary. Is it desirable?

18 NOVEMBER 1984

Miss A. M. Stratford, of King's Lynn in Norfolk, wrote: 'I was brought up to believe that a fundamental difference exists between "can" and "may", but your note suggests this is no longer so. As I quite often need to make this important

33

distinction I would appreciate guidance.' I was similarly brought up ('Can I go out and play?' 'Of course you can. The question is *"May* you"') and so were my children. This one is trickier. A conscientious deaconess is *physically* capable of saying 'you'. She would be professionally and morally incapable of doing so. It demonstrates, I think, the short-comings of hard and fast rules.

D EBRIEF, from 'de-' and 'to brief', caught a reader's attention in a Radio 4 news broadcast last month about the released American hostages in Lebanon. The OED shows that 'brief' first entered the language as a noun, from *breve* – letter, dispatch, note in late classical Latin, neuter of *brevis*, short. It soon passed into the Teutonic languages – in Dutch and German *brief* is still the current word for 'letter'. However, the entry goes on, 'it is not recorded in Old English, and appears to have entered Middle English [1100s to 1400s] from French. Here also it has remained more distinctly an official or legal word, and has not the sense of "letter".' The first OED definition (earliest example 1292) is 'a writing issued by official or legal authorities: a royal letter of mandate'. The verb is much later, first in the obsolete sense of to shorten (1601), then in its present sense of to brief a barrister (1832).

'Debrief' is a World War Two creation: 'The RAF use of the atrocity debrief. When airmen receive their orders for an operation, they are said to be briefed – a quite legitimate extension of the legal term. But when they return to give their report, they do not just report, as one would think. They are debriefed' – *John O'London's Weekly*, 16 November 1945, quoted in Volume II of A Supplement to the OED. The tone of the passage suggests unease about the word, but the writer has missed its implicit element of interrogation. Webster's Third New International (1961) defines it: 'To interrogate (as a pilot returning from a mission or a government official returning from abroad) in order to obtain useful information or intelligence.' Examples in the files of the Oxford English Dictionaries include: 'What will happen to Oleg Lyalin? What in fact happens to any Soviet defector who betrays his country for asylum? Lyalin is being debriefed by British intelligence under maximum security conditions. When the British are finished with him, America's Central Intelligence Agency will take a turn at interrogation' (*Sunday Mail Magazine*, Brisbane, 4 April 1983) and, 'Simko, his 34-year-old wife and their 12-year-old son, Sven, are now safe in a secret British retreat while he is being "debriefed" by British counter intelligence' (*Daily Telegraph*, 24 February 1977).

Two interesting examples from fiction: 'They had made it clear to him [the defecting British secret agent], particularly Ivan who had met his plane in Prague and accompanied him to a debriefing in some place near Irkutsk' (Graham Greene's *The Human Factor*). And, from Steven Spielberg's *Close Encounters of the Third Kind*: 'Lieutenant, welcome home,' says the master of ceremonies to a flier landing in a spaceship after wandering round the Universe for decades: 'This way to debriefing.' It never fails to raise a laugh from movie audiences.

11 AUGUST 1985

DEPRECATE/DEPRECIATE. The Rev Norman Leak

of Manchester writes: 'At a conference recently, a psychiatrist said that hospital chaplains "tended to be full of self-deprecation". I said to my neighbour: "surely he means 'self-depreciation'", only to be told I was wrong. But "self-deprecation", as I understand it, involves severe disapproval, even cursing, of oneself, whereas "self-depreciation" means running oneself down.'

'Deprecate', 'to express disapproval of', from Latin *deprecor*, originally meant 'to pray against'. The first OED definition of 'depreciate' (from *de*, down, and *pretium*, price) is 'to lower the value of', then, by extension, 'belittle'. Nowadays, as the Longman Dictionary of the English Language says, the two words 'are freely interchangeable'. That is a pity. A *Guardian* piece on Gooch's 129 runs in Trinidad last month had: 'Only one person was inclined to deprecate Gooch's performance: the lad himself.' The report then quoted Gooch as saying: 'Very flat wicket.' Mr Leak comments: 'I'm sure Gooch wasn't deploring his marvellous innings; he was simply undervaluing it, on the grounds that the wicket made it easier.'

But at least we know what Gooch meant. Take another example. A *London Review of Books* article on Horace Walpole's Memoirs (7 November 1985) had: 'Some [passages] are unconvincingly self-deprecating, as when he writes . . . "I am no

35

historian; I write casual memoirs . . . "'. Did the reviewer mean Walpole was expressing disapproval of himself as an historian (deprecation) or that he was 'representing himself as of less value than usually assigned' ('depreciation' in Webster's Collegiate)? I don't know. When Bernard Levin wrote in an *Observer* book review last November, 'Then he [E. M. Forster] begins to depreciate his own writing', one knew exactly what he meant.

20 APRIL 1986

Cambridge

DEAR MR SILVERLIGHT, Till you convince me that, for example, the statements

    (a) 'Chamberlain deprecated the German invasion of Poland on 1 September 1939'
    and
    (b) 'Chamberlain depreciated the German invasion . . . '

are not directly opposed in their meaning – by (a) he went on to declare war against Germany two days later; by (b) he would have stuck his ostrich-head once more into the sands – then you must NOT condone the slovenliness, supported by Longman's Dictionary as it may be, which elides 'deprecate' with 'depreciate'. For what it matters the Guardian *piece on Gooch would have been little less slovenly even had 'depreciate' been substituted for 'deprecate'. The* mot juste *was 'belittle'. Any halfway-to-good writer knows that when a word is used ambiguously, then you use a clearer word. The reviewer of Walpole meant that 'in some of the passages he unduly belittles himself . . . '*

DR D. T. WHITESIDE

DERRING-DO. A correspondent writes of his shock at seeing the word 'targeted' in this paper: 'Is "to target" really a verb? If so, what is to become of "to aim"?' The OED has an example of the verb 'target' dated 1837. I think it is a useful word: 'targeting' a nuclear missile sounds more positive, and so more sinister, than merely aiming it, but that is a subjective view. What is certain is that abusage, as they see it, arouses strong feelings in many people who care about the language. I wonder what their previous counterparts would have made of the evolution of the Middle English 'durryng don', meaning 'daring to do', in Chaucer's *Troilus and Criseyde* (1380s) into the 'derring-do' in Scott's *Ivanhoe* (1820), meaning 'desperate courage'?

'Derring-do' says the OED, 'is a pseudo-archaicism'. The change in sense took place thanks to 'a chain of misunderstandings and errors'. Chaucer wrote: 'Troilus was nevere . . . secounde/In durrynge don that longeth to a knyght . . . ' In that passage 'the words come in their ordinary sense and construction followed by the object "that" (= what)'. In 1430, John Lydgate, an admirer of Chaucer, wrote 'in an imitative passage' and 'a construction more liable to misunderstanding': 'And paregal [fully equal] . . . he [Troilus] was to any . . . / In dorrynge do.' A century and a half later, and now spelled 'derring doe', it was picked up by Spenser and misconstrued as 'manhood and chivalry'. The note ends, 'Modern Romantic writers, led by Sir W. Scott, have . . . accentuated the erroneous use.'

(That word 'abusage' in the first paragraph above – was it, I wondered, coined by Eric Partridge? It is in the OED, but is shown as 'obs.' (entry prepared in 1884); the last example is dated 1649. Vol. I of A Supplement has: 'Revived 1942 E. Partridge: "Usage and abusage. A guide to good English".')

24 NOVEMBER 1985

D OG DAYS, a literal translation of the Greek *hemerai kynades* (Latin *dies caniculares*), are 'about the time of the heliacal rising of the Dog Star; noted from ancient times as the hottest and most unwholesome time of the year', the season at which, it was popularly believed, 'dogs are most apt to run mad' – OED. We are just about in the middle of them. 'In current almanacks,' the entry says, 'they are said to begin July 3 and end Aug. 11.' The 'heliacal rising' of a star is its first appearance of the season in the twilight just before sunrise, as distinct from its 'cosmical rising', which coincides with the sunrise itself and so cannot be observed visually; its time is calculated mathematically.

Ancient Egyptians took a different view of the Dog Star, or Sirius as it is usually known. They noted that its heliacal rising coincided with the annual flooding of the Nile; to them it was the 'creator of all green growing things' – *Britannica*, quoting a Pyramid text. (They also observed that the heliacal risings of Sirius took place at intervals of 365¼ days, not the 365 days of their calendar year. Julius Caesar incorporated the correction in his reform of the Roman calendar with his leap years.) The Greek poet Hesiod (fl. about 800 BC; he is generally regarded as being a little later than Homer), in the epic poem *Works and Days* – his instructions to farmers – describes the Dog Days as the time when 'women are at their most wanton, but men are feeblest, because Sirius parches head and knees and the skin is dry through heat'. 'Sirius', cognate with the Greek *seirioeis*, scorching, may go back to an Indo-European word for 'sparkling'. Hardy writes in *Far from the Madding Crowd* of 'the kingly brilliance of Sirius'. It is indeed the brightest star in the firmament, 20 times as luminous as the sun.

I have also just learnt that 'cynosure' ('The fair young Queen . . . cynosure of all eyes' – Carlyle's *French Revolution*, 1837) comes from the Greek *kynosoura*, dog's tail. The OED's first definition is: 'The northern constellation Ursa Minor, which contains in its tail the Pole Star'.

22 JULY 1984

ECU. Last week *The Times*, editorialising about the Greek Prime Minister Mr Papandreou's demands on the EEC, said they amounted to '5,000 ecus (or £3,000)'. I had not heard of an 'ecu' – nor had several colleagues – but it stands for European Currency Unit. Whether by coincidence or not, an *écu* was an old French silver coin (the word is derived from the Latin *scutum*, a shield), *'valant'*, says the *Petit Larousse*, '3 livres . . . Saint Louis [Louis IX, 1214–70] fit frapper les premiers écus.'

9 DECEMBER 1984

Mondorf-les-Bains, Luxembourg

DEAR MR SILVERLIGHT, *It is no coincidence that the European Currency Unit is called the* écu, *at any rate in French: that was the deliberate* astuce *of Helmut Schmidt, the German Chancellor, and Giscard d'Estaing, the French President, when this amazingly*

38

successful little financial object was brought into being at the Summit Meeting of Bremen in 1978. (Remember that Helmut and Giscard, curiously enough, had the habit of conversing in English!) Giscard could sell the idea to his countrymen just because it evoked the glories of old France.

The écu has been vigorously adopted as a currency in its own right by especially the Belgians, the Italians and the French, for stock issues and trade credit; ironically, it is only the Germans who won't play ball with it. There are now even passbooks for savings accounts and travellers' cheques denominated in ECUs. In England it is still rather suspect or unknown, but it is the precursor of a common European currency.

Yours sincerely

ANTHONY CLOVER

Monks Kirby, Warwickshire

DEAR SIR, *I was devastated to read in* The Observer *on 9 December your comment that* The Times *was 'editorialising about . . . '*

Yours faithfully

S. PETTIFER

I used the word unthinkingly and I suppose it was not very pretty. However, it exactly and economically expresses my meaning. By themselves 'wrote', 'said', 'commented' would have been inadequate; to add 'in an editorial' would have taken more space (and would have been slightly portentous in so slight a piece). The verb admittedly originated in the United States, but I think it is a legitimate back-formation from 'editorial', which I prefer to 'leader' or 'leading article', and *is* English in origin. The OED's first example reads: 'Mr Bennett . . . thinks that "an editorial" is the highest style of composition known' – *Spectator*, 1864.

EGREGIOUS. Even the most crassly self-satisfied Roman would surely have felt flattered to be described as *egregius* (from *e*, out, and *grex*, flock, 'hence', says the OED, 'towering

above the flock'). Among synonyms in Lewis and Short is *praeclarus*, very beautiful (physically and morally), splendid, noble etc. Under the Empire, to be styled *Egregius* was a perk of high office, the almost exact equivalent of 'His Excellency'. The word has fared less well in English. 'Egregious', Thomas Nashe wrote in 1593, 'never used in english but in the extreame ill parte.' 'Italian fiend!', 'Egregious murderer' are the imprecations Posthumus hurls at Iachimo in *Cymbeline*.

At that time Nashe's 'never' was not yet quite right. An OED example with 'egregious' in the now obsolete sense of distinguished, eminent, excellent, renowned, is dated 1534; and there is one dated as late as 1855 – 'some one egregious and splendid' (Thackeray, in *The Newcomes*). But Nashe clearly sensed what was happening to the word. The OED's first example with the bad sense – gross, flagrant, outrageous – is: 'Thai them selvs cannot dissemble it without egregius impudenci' (1553). An example with the adverb is earlier still: 'Here have I blotted your Paper vainly, and played the fool egregiously' – Bishop Latimer in 1555, the year he was burnt with Ridley and Cranmer at Oxford, quoted in Foxe's *Book of Martyrs* (Milton figures among both sets of examples: 'This is egregious doctrine, and for which charity will thank them', 1645; 'Egregious Liars and Impostors', 1648). The 'bad' sense, says the OED, probably arose from an ironical use of the 'good' senses, 'though our earliest quotations afford no evidence of this'. I take it as just one more example of the mysterious ways of usage.

15 SEPTEMBER 1985

Edinburgh

DEAR JOHN SILVERLIGHT, *It's perhaps a bit inaccurate to imply that Latin* egregius *was invariably flattering. If 'egregious' could be used ironically (OED, as you report, adduces this use as the source of the present wholly derogatory meaning), then so could* egregius. *A good example is Virgil,* Aeneid *VI, 523, where the shade of Deiphobus relates how, at the fall of Troy, his* egregia coniunx, *(his 'excellent wife', Lacaena) had removed all his weapons, so that he could not defend himself against the Greeks. Other Latin authors from Cicero to St Augustine used* egregius *sarcastically.*

Of course, it's one thing for a laudatory adjective to be used ironically and quite another for it to be used to qualify something manifestly bad, as 'liar', 'ass', etc. (i.e. the meaning 'flagrant', 'gross', 'outrageous' that 'egregious' has today). I'm not sure, however, that egregius was positively never used in this way. We have, for instance, in Aulus Gellius (13, 31, 13), the phrase ille egregius nebulo, which appears to mean 'that egregious fool'.

Yours sincerely

ANNE SEATON

Sources: Oxford Latin Dictionary; *Thesaurus Linguae Latinae*.

EMBER DAYS.

Among matters dealt with by the Council of Placentia (modern Piacenza) in 1095 was an appeal from the Emperor of Byzantium for aid against the Turks. Another was fixing the dates of Ember Days, the Church's 'four periods of fasting and prayer (Latin *quattuor tempora*) to be observed at the four seasons' according to the OED. Whether or not the Byzantine appeal was successful, Constantinople fell in 1453. The dates of Ember Days have only recently been changed. In the late 1970s a new Church of England calendar was authorised, making the dates coincide with the end of college terms – clergy are traditionally ordained at Ember seasons – and churches that follow the Alternative Services Book as distinct from the Book of Common Prayer observe the new dates. The *days* remain the same, Wednesday, Friday and Saturday, but the winter 'season', for instance, has been moved to the week *before* the Third Sunday in Advent (which this year is today) from the week *after* St Lucy's Day, 13 December. (John Donne's poem *A Nocturnall Upon S. Lucies Day* is subtitled 'Being the Shortest Day of the Year'. Really? 13 December? Yes: in 1752 the Gregorian Calendar succeeded the Julian Calendar and 11 days were lost. In Donne's time it would have been the shortest day or very nearly so.)

Dictionaries say that 'ember' in this sense, as distinct from fragments of a dying fire, derives from Old English *ymbryne*, circuit, i.e. of the seasons. But the OED says that it is also 'not impossible that the word may be due to popular etymology working upon some Vulgar Latin corruption of *quattuor tempora*'.

15 DECEMBER 1985

EMULATE. I think lexicographers are out of step on this one. The Concise Oxford's 'to try to equal or excel; rival; imitate zealously' is typical. Admittedly it follows translations of *aemulor* in Latin-English dictionaries, but only in the 'bad' sense, to be envious, or jealous. *Aemulor* also has a 'good' sense, to be emulous of glory, or praise. So does *aemulatio*, emulation, unlike *rivalitas*, which has only a bad sense, jealous rivalry. (It comes from *rivus*, brook; *rivales* are people who use the same brook, neighbours – Israel, Jordan and the River Jordan come to mind. By extension, *rivalis* is someone with the same mistress.) Anyway, Latin usage does not necessarily determine English usage. Definitions of 'emulate', with their emphasis on rivalry, fail to bring out the word's hint of generous admiration, something of Tennyson's 'We needs must love the highest when we see it' (Guinevere, in *Idylls of the King*, lamenting her infidelity to Arthur). Dryden has it right: 'Condemn the bad, and Emulate the good.'

20 OCTOBER 1985

ENORMITY. 'Some people', says Webster's New Collegiate (ninth edition, 1983), insist that the word 'is improperly used to denote large size and is properly used only to denote wickedness'. But '"enormity" is used with more subtleness than is usu. indicated . . . it need not carry overtones of moral transgression, although it most often does'. Here are two examples of this 'more subtle' use. In the *Listener* of 28 June Peter Taylor writes of the 'enormity' of the heroin problem in this country. As a good writer (he is the author of *Smoke Ring: the Politics of Tobacco*) he is aware of the 'correct' use of the word. The moral transgression, he told me, 'is on the part of the pushers'. Three days later, in *A Captive Lion*, a Radio 3 biography of the Russian poet Maria Tsvetayeva, by Elaine Feinstein, I heard the phrase 'the enormity of his need to be loved'. Extent, of course, but something more as well. 'There was something sick about the need,' Miss Feinstein said on the telephone.

Another target of purists is the use of 'flaunt' for 'flout'. This, says Webster's, 'cannot be called substandard', though 'many people will consider it a mistake'. Mr J. M. Smith, of

West Kirby, Merseyside, points out that an advertisement in *The Observer Colour Magazine* last Sunday says 'drivers widely flaunt it [the speed limit]'. Not such a distinguished example as the ones for 'enormity', but a straw in the wind.

8 JULY 1984

E̲PHEMERA. Last month I came across this word three times in three weeks: 'Professor Trevor-Roper has reprinted a collection of ephemera' – *London Review of Books*, 7 November; ' . . . cartoons, posters and other ephemera' – *The Observer*, 17 November; 'Among my prized ephemera is a copy of the January 1939 *Journal of the British Interplanetary Society*' – *Listener*, 28 November. It derives from the Greek *hemera*, day, via the related adjective *ephemeros*, short-lived, transitory. The neuter, i.e. a short-lived thing, is *ephemeron*, of which the plural is *ephemera*, whence the above examples. In dictionaries, however, 'ephemera' is shown first in the sense of an insect, the mayfly, and as a *singular*; the plural is 'ephemeras' or 'ephemerae'. I found this confusing.

The Chambers 'ephemera' entry is the most helpful: 'an insect of this genus . . . but see also "ephemeron" below'. There, after 'insect' etc., is ' . . . usu. in plural, an object of no value'. (So much for journalism, incidentally; the modern Greek word for 'newspaper' is *ephemerida*.) The singular 'ephemera' comes from a Late Latin adaptation of the Greek adjective. (The first 'e' in *hemera* is long, and classical scholars pronounce the English derivative *epheemera*; dictionaries, including the big Oxford, show it with a short second 'e'. 'So much the worse for the Oxford English Dictionary', said one such scholar.)

A related word is 'ephemeris' (transcribed from the Greek for diary): a table giving the position of celestial objects such as Halley's Comet (as with 'ephemera', dictionaries show 'ephemeris' with a short second 'e'; astronomers say *epheemeris*). Ephemerides are essential for navigators and astronomers, and the oldest current national publication is the *Connaissance des temps*, founded in Paris in 1679 'as the direct successor of ephemerides begun by the German astrologer Johannes Kepler in 1617' (*Britannica*). *The British Nautical Almanac and Astronomical*

43

Ephemeris, now entitled *The Astronomical Almanac*, was founded in 1767.

29 DECEMBER 1985

E̲TIQUETTE/PROTOCOL. Friends of mine recently received a beautifully engraved invitation card saying, 'The Lord Chamberlain is commanded by Her Majesty to invite Mr and Mrs St. John Jones [not their real name] to a Garden Party at Buckingham Palace on Tuesday 10th July 1984 . . . ' When I expressed surprise that the envelope was addressed 'Mrs St. J. J.' rather than 'Mr and Mrs' I was told, 'Oh, but the invitation is always sent to the wife': it is the woman who, it is assumed, handles a couple's social affairs. Is all this (leaving aside the importance or otherwise of the issue) to do with etiquette or protocol? My immediate, not very well-informed guess was the former. However . . .

'Etiquette' of course means 'conventional rules of personal behaviour in polite society' (Concise Oxford). But the OED's first – and still current – definition is, besides 'prescribed ceremonial of a court', the 'formalities required by usage in diplomatic intercourse'. 'Protocol' (from a Greek word meaning first sheet of a papyrus roll, bearing the maker's mark) first meant 'original note of a transaction' etc., drawn up by a public official, 'which forms the legal authority for any subsequent deed' etc. (OED). Next comes 'original draft' of, say, a treaty. By the nineteenth century one of its senses in France was the etiquette department of the Foreign Ministry. So to its present 'extended and general uses, any code or convention of proper conduct; formally correct behaviour' (Vol. III of A Supplement to the OED). The addressing of invitations does have more to do with etiquette than protocol, but the two words are much closer to each other than I thought.

24 JUNE 1984

E̲UPHEMISM: 'An inoffensive word or phrase substituted for one considered offensive or hurtful, esp. one concerned with religion, sex, death or excreta. Examples: "sleep with" for "have sexual intercourse with"; "departed" for "dead"; "relieve oneself" for "urinate"' – Collins, a useful, comprehensive definition. To use a euphemism is not just to be mealy-mouthed. I believe it reflects a basic conflict in all of us that goes back to the emergence of speech: between the wish to express oneself strongly and the wish not to offend fellow mortals, let alone the immortals. The Greeks not only coined the word ('euphemism' derives from *eu*, good, and *pheme*, speech); they also coined the archetypal example, the Eumenides, the Kindly Ones, the alternative Greek word for the Furies.

In some eras, permissivists prevail; in others, restrictivists. We are more permissive than the Victorians. So were the Elizabethans. In much present-day fiction and drama, it is difficult to see how permissiveness can go much further. But what about the Press? Shortly after I joined *The Observer*, in the early 1960s, we used the most famous four-letter word of all in a piece on the *Lady Chatterley's Lover* trial. There were dire warnings from colleagues in the commercial and advertising departments, but it did no harm that one could see. However, and here is the point, nor did it open the floodgates of unlimited obscenity: more than 20 years later, the word rarely appears in *The Observer* or any other quality paper. And although I may have missed it, I have yet to see it in a mass circulation paper.

Modern dictionaries give those words – but always with a warning. The 1938 Cassells French dictionary translates *le mot de Cambronne* (see NO SURRENDER) as 'You be blowed!' Very funny. The 1984 Collins–Robert has 'Hells bells!' Not a very daring or deep descent. The *Grand Larousse* dictionary has the word itself, of course. The *Grand Larousse* encyclopaedia in its Cambronne entry has only: 'the energetic word that made him famous'.

24 MARCH 1985

FALSE FRIENDS. A *faux ami* is 'a word in a foreign

language that does not mean what it appears to, e.g. in Italian *pretendere* does not mean "to pretend"' – Chambers (it means 'to claim', as in Old Pretender). C. M. Woodhouse, classical scholar and historian (his latest book is *The Rise and Fall of the Greek Colonels*), has sent us two examples involving modern Greek. In a recent article in *The Times* defending sociology as an academic discipline, Dr David Martin of the London School of Economics and Political Science cited authorities including Aristotle and Montesquieu and claimed that only idiots – 'in the strict Greek sense of the word' – could ignore them. However, 'in the strict Greek sense' *idiótes* did not mean 'fool', as Professor Martin's use of 'idiot' suggests: it meant a private citizen as distinct from soneone involved in politics. Later, Mr Woodhouse writes, 'it came to mean a layman, inexpert, and therefore eventually a fool. In modern Greek the word *idiótes* has reverted to its original meaning. Thus the adjective *idiotikòs* does not mean "idiotic", but "private" as distinct from official. In 1940 the basements of buildings all over Athens were labelled *idiotikòn kataphýgiòn*, meaning "private citizens' air raid shelter". Fortunately Athens was never bombed, but that did not make the precaution idiotic. Etymologically, the word "atomic" means the same as "individual", and that is the normal meaning of the Greek *átomon*. Similarly, *atomikòs* means "pertaining to the individual", as in the army phrase *atomikì bómba*, "hand grenade". I recall vividly the amazement caused in Athens in August 1945 by the news that the Japanese had surrendered after the dropping of two "hand grenades"!'

(I like the notice in a small hotel in Crete that, after half a dozen visits, I still read as 'Only three atoms allowed in this lift.')

16 FEBRUARY 1986

FOETUS/FETUS.

Mr John McGarry, of Bittadon in Devon, a consultant gynaecologist, questions my spelling of 'foetus' in *Words* of 6 January 1980, which he read in the collected columns published in 1985. He sent along evidence. In the *Lancet* of 29 November 1969 a letter begins: 'I never thought that you would treat us/To transatlantic words like "fetus"'; and a footnote reads: 'We're grateful for your letter/But the form with "e" is better. – Ed. *L*.' in the *British Medical Journal* of 7 September 1985 a correspondent writes that 'fetus' 'is the correct English spelling'.

It comes from Latin *feto*, to bring forth, and the OED (entry prepared for publication in 1897) says that 'fetus' is the 'etymologically preferred spelling . . . but in actual use is almost unknown'. In the Shorter Oxford (1933) it is still 'almost unknown'; the Concise (1982) shows 'fetus' as 'chiefly US'. My bet is that 'fetus', however 'correct', will continue almost unknown.

I was also interested to discover that the preferred spelling of 'fetid' is etymologically unsound too – because it *lacks* an 'o'. The OED shows it deriving from the Latin word of the same sense, foul-smelling, which it gives as *'fetidus*, often incorrectly written *foetidus'*. This is in accord with the great Lewis and Short Latin Dictionary, which, however, was published in 1879. The Oxford Latin Dictionary, published in 1968–82, has *foetidus*, and a classical scholar I consulted, the publisher Colin Haycraft, thinks this spelling should be preferred. Theoretically, then, 'foetid' should be preferred too, but of course it won't be (which is why I put 'correct' in quotation marks when discussing 'fetus').

On the pronunciation of 'fetid', classical scholars like a long 'e', but most dictionaries give short 'e' first; an exception is Chambers. The Longman Dictionary of the English Language says short 'e' is recommended for BBC broadcasters 'except when the word is spelt "foetid"'.

6 APRIL 1986

DEAR MR SILVERLIGHT, May I suggest that unless you place some restriction on your bet that 'fetus will continue almost unknown' it is lost already. It is almost universal among the people who use it most: the gynaecologists, the obstetricians and the nursing staffs at all levels. I serve as a volunteer in our local School of Midwifery and it has added to my interest to abstract from the catalogue thirty books: twenty-five use 'fetus'. [Representative titles are: Stedman's Medical Dictionary, Modern Obstetrics, Midwifery, Midwives Dictionary, The Newborn Child, Book of Child Care – JS.]

Since these books include works by some of the most eminent men and women in this field, it is reasonable to assume that the practitioners are somewhat ahead of the producers of more general dictionaries. You are further asked to accept that this is not a biased list but has been taken on a general run-through along the shelves.

Yours sincerely

JOHN ROBERTS

DEAR JOHN SILVERLIGHT, I suspect that you have not reckoned on the influence of the various international bodies which exist to standardise the terminology used by medical scientists. These committees appear to have a paranoid fear of diphthongs; as a clinical biochemist I have recently had to follow an IFCC (International Federation of Clinical Chemists) ruling that 'oestrogen' is obsolete and that the ugly 'estrogen' is to be preferred. Pathologists, by and large, stick with the guidelines issued by the CAP (College of American Pathologists). They naturally prefer 'fetus'. I have looked at both the standard pathology texts that I have at home; both are English and both give 'fetus' without even suggesting 'foetus' as an alternative. The books are The Language of Pathology, *by Glyn Walters (1979) and* An Introduction to General Pathology, *by W. G. Spector (1980).*

Yours sincerely

SUE PERKS

Those letters, so authoritative and moderate in tone, make me regret what I now recognise as cockiness (I forgot my proper role in matters of usage – that of a reporter, not an expert). I do not entirely retract what I wrote, but in retrospect I wish I had said something like, ' . . . my feeling is that "foetus" will continue to be so spelt for some years if not decades'. (It is also absurd to describe the spelling 'fetus' as 'almost unknown'. In 1897, perhaps; not in 1986.)

I base my feeling on the fact that people are deeply conservative where change in usage is concerned. Admittedly there is the influence of American usage, but look at how, say, the 'u' in 'colour' has persisted. The different factor in 'foetus' v. 'fetus' is that practically the whole medical profession – a small but not inconsiderable proportion of the population – is committed to the latter. But usage does not change at the behest of specialists. Lexicographers (who, incidentally, being people too, are on the whole also conservative) have no doubt taken notice of the change in specialist usage. But as practitioners they react to change in *general* usage, especially, I suspect, 'educated' general usage. I further suspect that the 'educated' in our society prefer 'foetus'. I still think it will be some time before 'fetus' appears in dictionaries as the preferred spelling.

F̶RIEND: 'One loving or attached to another' (Chambers); 'a person whose company, interests and attitudes one finds sympathetic and to whom one is not related' (Longman); 'a person known well and regarded with liking, affection and loyalty' (Collins); 'one joined to another in intimacy and mutual benevolence independently of sexual or family love' (Concise Oxford).

I like all those definitions, especially Collins's, with its 'loyalty'. But my favourite is Oxford's, with its faintly and beguilingly archaic phrasing. So to the big Oxford. It's all very interesting. Except that 'intimacy' and 'mutual benevolence' are transposed, the first definition is exactly the same as in the Concise. It is, however, in quotation marks and is followed by '(J)'. The OED of course has many references to Dr Johnson, but I have not seen one like that elsewhere. (Incidentally, the 1982 Concise definition is also exactly the same as in the 1934 edition, the last for which H. W. Fowler was responsible.)

The OED entry continues: 'Not ordinarily applied to lovers or relatives (but see senses 3,4).' Sense 3 is 'A kinsman or near relation' (which Chambers shows as still a current sense in Scots English). Sense 4 is 'A lover or paramour of either sex. *Obs.*': 'He hath got his friend with child' (*Measure for Measure*); 'When a gentleman wanted a friend, I could supply him with a choice in an hour' (*The Commissary*, by Samuel Foot, 1764). Longman also has this sense, also labelled '*Obs*'. But, and this is what I find most interesting, those '*obs.*' labels are themselves obsolete. Volume I of A Supplement to the OED has, under 'friend', 'delete *obs.* and add later examples'. The first is 'friend, the man who keeps a harlot as his mistress' (Partridge's *Dictionary of Quotations*). Just good friends? (See ACQUAINTANCE.)

21 SEPTEMBER 1986

G̶ALLANT. A word I have taken too much for granted. Gallantry in battle, of course. 'A very gallant gentleman' – Captain Oates's epitaph inscribed by two of his companions in the Antarctic on the cross marking the approximate place of his death. 'The hon. and gallant gentleman' – parliamentese for an MP who holds a commission in the Armed Forces. A gallant ship. A man of fashion and pleasure.

I was less familiar with those senses of the word that stress the second syllable. In front of me in a florist's the other day were a youngish, very attractive woman and a not-so-young man. The florist made as if to serve the man, who said, indicating the woman, 'This lady was before me.' 'Thank you,' she replied, 'how gallant [*gallánt*] of you.' Here was the sense 'markedly polite to the female sex'. Another definition in this group is 'of or pertaining to (sexual) love, amorous, amatory', but such usages are less common in English than in French, to judge from a comparison of material in the OED and the *Grand Larousse de la Langue Française*. *Femme galante* means 'woman of light morals'; *vert galant* is a man who is *entreprenant* (enterprising) *avec les femmes*; the synonym of the noun *galant* is *coureur*, womaniser; synonyms of *galante* are *courtisane, hétaire*. As with 'malignant' (see entry), I feel that all this tells us something about the difference between the French and the English. German has an ominous colloquial usage that gives warning of what gallantry, in the sense of amorous trifling, can lead to: *galante Krankheit*, literally gallant disease, means syphilis.

On a lighter note, there is also the sense in music. On the same day as the exchange of civilities in the florist's shop I heard Fritz Spiegl on Radio 3 describe Mozart's *Les Petits Riens* (composed in 1778) as 'the embodiment of the gallant style'. This style is sometimes dismissed as 'elegant but superficial'. Perhaps it is. However, Voltaire, quoted in the *style galant* entry in Grove's Musical Dictionary, wrote, 'Being *galant*, in general, means seeking to please.' The *style galant* entirely succeeds in doing just that.

2 JUNE 1985

G̲AOL/JAIL: which is 'correct'? The latest edition of *The Oxford Dictionary for Writers and Editors* (1981, reprinted with corrections 1982) has '**gaol**, *not* jail'. That puzzles me, as does the latest Concise (1982), with its '**g**- in official use, **g**- and **j**- in literary use . . . '. Here the Concise is following the OED's 'gaol' entry, published in 1898, but it omits the OED's description of 'gaol' as a variant of 'jail' and the observation that 'all recent dictionaries give the precedence to "jail"'.

Instead, unlike the OED, the Concise gives precedence to 'gaol'.

The OED's 'jail' entry has a longish etymological and historical note, which shows it deriving from Old French *jaiole*. It describes the spelling 'gaol' as 'archaic' and 'obsolete in the spoken language'. Examples include 'Carrie this mad knaue to the Iaile' (*Taming of the Shrew*). But as far as I can see there is something even more significant. By 1898, let alone 1982, 'gaol' was obsolete officially as well as 'in the spoken language' if, as I take it, 'officially' means in official written usage. An official in the Prison Service Press Office says that prisons used indeed to be known as 'gaols', for example Bedford County Gaol and Birmingham City Gaol. But since the latter half of the nineteenth century, after the formation of the Prison Commission, only the word 'prison' has been used. He would never speak of 'gaol' ('jail'?) except loosely.

The 'gaol' entry in the first edition of Fowler (1926) ends by saying that there is 'a strong argument for writing "jail"'. So does the second edition (1965). The Concise Oxford and Writers' and Editors' dictionaries seem not to agree. *The Observer*, like most other papers, uses 'jail'.

12 OCTOBER 1986

GRACILE – Clive James's description of Concorde in *The Observer* last month. I did not know the word, but its sound and context suggested that its sense was approbatory and this was confirmed by dictionaries: gracefully slender is the sense generally given. (I wonder, irrelevantly, if Mr James would so approve of the plane if, like me, he lived under its flight path.) The Latin word it comes from, *gracilis*, is cognate with a Sanskrit verb meaning to be lean, old. Besides slight and slender its meanings include meagre, lean, scanty, poor. Seutonius vividly describes Nero as having a protruding belly (*ventri proiecto*) and very thin legs (*gracillimis cruribus*), which is hardly a compliment. In contrast Horace writes in one of his Odes: '*Quis multa gracilis te puer in rosa/perfusus liquidis urget odoribus/grato, Pyrrha, sub antro?*' 'What slender boy, drenched in perfume, woos you, Pyrrha, on a bed of roses in a seductive grotto?' Ovid, in his *Remedia Amoris*, advises the unsuccessful lover: 'Call her fat if she is full-breasted, black if dark-complexioned; in a slender woman (*gracilis*) leanness can be a reproach.' Usually the word has the neutral sense of thin.

Something of all this comes across in the OED definition 'Slender, thin, lean'. One example reads: 'Unswathe his Egyptian mummy and . . . you disclose the grave features and gracile bones . . . of a cat' – Walter Savage Landor (1824). There is also this note: 'By some recent writers [entry ready for publication in 1900] misused, through association with "grace", for "gracefully slender".' An example reads, 'Girls . . . beautiful with the beauty of ruddy bronze, gracile as the palmettoes that sway above them' – *Harper's Magazine*, April 1888. That 'misuse' is now fully accepted, to judge from modern dictionaries – according to Collins it can even mean 'graceful'. All the derogatory connotations have been shed: only Webster's New Collegiate reminds us of them – *gracilis*, it says, 'is akin to Old Norse *horr*, starvation'. It is an interesting example of amelioration, the change for the better in a word's meaning.

12 AUGUST 1984

HACKER. Stories of teenage computer pirates who use their

home computers to break into electronic files and 'mailboxes' are surfacing more and more often, notably last autumn when a message was inserted into Prince Philip's 'mailbox': 'I do so enjoy puzzles and games. Ta! Ta! Pip!!' However, I keep meeting people (including a computer scientist's wife), otherwise well informed, who haven't heard of the word 'hacker'. Not that I have known it long – only since last summer, when a colleague suggested that I should write about it (I didn't). The earliest example in print in the files of the Oxford Dictionaries is ' . . . a hacker is someone who spends much of his time writing computer programs' – *Scientific American*, October 1982.

That neutral sense did not last. The quarterly Barnhart Dictionary Companion for autumn 1983 defines 'hacker' as someone 'who seeks to gain unauthorised access to a computer system through a telephone connection'. According to *Inc.* of December 1983, few people were aware 'last year' of the problem. 'Then came the movie *War Games* and a rush of long-distance, electronic break-ins by a group of computer-literate teenagers, or "hackers", from Milwaukee.' *War Games* did indeed publicise hacking. It shows how a boy proceeds from 'accessing' (that word *is* in modern dictionaries, unlike 'hacker') the school computer, in order to change his girlfriend's 'F' in biology into an 'A', to tuning into the NORAD (North American Air Defence) holy of holies and bringing the world to the point of nuclear holocaust. The Pentagon insists that its system is utterly secure, that nothing like *War Games* could happen. But in December, after the Prince Philip incident, the *Daily Telegraph* interviewed 'Martin', a teenage hacker who said: 'As long as computer systems are designed by human beings, then, given time and patience, humans will break into them.'

24 FEBRUARY 1985

H AL/HARRY.

If, as some people would like, Prince Henry comes to be known as Prince Harry, will he also be called Prince Hal? My lexicographer friend John Ayto notes the ancient ancestry of both pet names. '"Cry God for Harry, England and St George!" cried Shakespeare's Henry V. The "Harry" noble was a gold coin in Henry VI's time. One of Henry VIII's men-of-war was the Great Harry. "Hal" seems to have been around just as early: in his profligate youth Henry V was Prince Hal, and Henry VIII was "Bluff King Hal". Which brings us to the interesting substitution of "l" for "r". We got Sally from Sarah, Dolly from Dorothy and Milly (and Polly) from Mary. And now television has familiarised us with two more: "Tel" (Terence) from *Minder* and "Del Boy" from *Only Fools and Horses*.'

21 APRIL 1985

Preston

DEAR SIR, *Another common substitution for 'r', in this part of the country at least, is that of 'z'. Examples are 'Kaz', 'Shaz', 'Baz' and 'Waz' for Karen, Sharon, Barry, and Warwick, and the latest, 'soz' for sorry.*

Yours faithfully

J. B. READER

HANDCUFF.

A. L. Wyman, of Barnes in south-west London, has sent in two newspaper cuttings illustrating what he describes as the apparent difficulty of 'describing the way someone is tied up'. One says the Nigerian victim of the attempted kidnapping earlier this month, Dr Dikko, was discovered in a crate at Stansted Airport 'kneeling with his ankles handcuffed together'. 'This seems a very acrobatic feat,' Mr Wyman comments. The other reads, 'Then the Great Houdini would be handcuffed, manacled . . . and lowered into the East River.' What is the difference? I can see the objection to describing ankles as being *hand*cuffed. Mr Wyman suggests that 'fettered' is what the writer means – 'fetter' is a form of the Old Teutonic word for foot. But although more logical, 'fettered' sounds old-fashioned to me. Logically 'manacled' is no better. Derived from the Latin *manicula*, little hand, strictly it means a fetter for the hand, handcuffed; anyway I find 'manacled' dated too. 'Shackle', which may come from an old word for link, would do since it has nothing to do with hand, but yet again it isn't a word that comes easily to mind. Perhaps handcuffed is as good as any. At least the word suggests something that can be adjusted to fit varying sizes of limb.

To handcuff, says the OED, comes from the noun 'hand' and the verb 'cuff' in the sense 'to put cuffs on', which it describes as rare. Not in the US. 'Cuff him,' one New York cop tells another in a science-fiction novel full (relentlessly so) of modern American usage, and the suspect is duly handcuffed (*Mission* by Patrick Tilley, 1981). Webster's Collegiate gives the definition 'to handcuff' for the verb 'cuff' before 'to strike with the open palm', the only one given in British desk dictionaries.

29 JULY 1984

HANDSAW.

The narrator in Julian Barnes's novel *Flaubert's Parrot* tells of a lecture 'by a professor from Cambridge' on 'Mistakes in Literature and Whether They Matter'. 'Yevtushenko, for example, apparently, made a howler in one of his poems about the American nightingale. Pushkin was quite wrong about the sort of military dress worn at balls . . . Nabokov was wrong – rather surprising this – about the phonetics of the name Lolita. There were other examples:

Coleridge, Yeats and Browning were some of those caught out not knowing a hawk from a handsaw, or not even knowing what a handsaw was in the first place.'

The reader goes along with the narrator in not thinking much of the professor: 'it was a very shiny performance. His bald head was shiny; his black shoes were shiny; and his lecture was very shiny indeed.' However, the pedant in me was worried by 'handsaw'. I remembered from schooldays that it is one of Shakespeare's more famous obscurities – Hamlet's 'I am but mad north-north-west; when the wind is southerly, I know a hawk from a handsaw' – but I had forgotten, if I ever knew, what a handsaw was in that context. My Shakespeare is not annotated, and most desk dictionaries merely confirm that a handsaw is a saw 'operated with one hand'. An exception is Chambers, which adds 'perh. heronshaw, Shak.' The Concise Oxford is more helpful still. In the 'handsaw' entry is 'cf. "hawk"', and that entry explains that 'handsaw' may be a corruption of 'hernshaw' or heron; the expression is defined as, 'to have ordinary discernment'. The 1953 Oxford Dictionary of Quotations has a footnote explaining 'handsaw'. The latest edition (1979) does not.

20 JULY 1985

Not even 'loo', a couple of years ago, provoked as many letters as Hamlet's 'I know a hawk from a handsaw' and the explanation that 'handsaw' was probably a corruption of 'heronshaw'. Laura Webster of Nottingham writes: 'Mr Silverlight will find that a visit to his DIY shop should provide both hawk and handsaw ("hawk, plasterer's square board with handle underneath" – Concise Oxford). Strange that while "everybody" knows what "Tudor" houses look like, with their timber construction and plaster infills, the tools essential to their building should give so much trouble to the professors.' Some readers provided helpful drawings. Two sent photocopies of illustrated catalogues of tool merchants. (One, from the 1958 Buck and Hickman catalogue, showed a 'Plasterer's Hawk, Made from Mild Yellow Pine, Size 12" × 12", Price 13s. 10d.' The firm still sells plasterer's hawks but only, alas, in aluminium, price £7.82.) To my shame I hadn't heard of a plasterer's hawk, but nor had colleagues, including Julian Barnes, who worked for some years with the Oxford Dictionaries, and whose novel *Flaubert's Parrot* originally prompted my piece.

55

Most of the letters were along similar lines, but a sizeable number, in support of the falconry metaphor, pointed out that the East Anglian dialect word for heron is 'harnser' which, especially with a slight flattening of the first 'r', does indeed sound like 'handsaw'. (Among these letters I particularly liked one from Mr Michael Hurst, of Newark in Nottinghamshire, who wrote: 'About fifteen or so years ago a journalist on the *Eastern Daily Press* called Eric Fowler, who wrote a weekly column under the *nom-de-guerre* Jonathan Mardle, produced a book called *Broad Norfolk*, in which he suggested that Hamlet's "handsaw" was probably the Norfolk harnser.' The *Eastern Daily Press* gave me my first job in journalism. Eric Fowler was the person there I came to know best. 'To mardle' is Norfolk for 'to gossip'.)

Harold Jenkins, in the Arden edition of *Hamlet* which he edited, accepts both explanations as plausible. However, the expression is a variation of a common type of proverbial phrase, and 'proverbs often delight to join incongruous items' and 'alliteration is quite as important as likeness and unlikeness . . . '. It is not necessary to suppose that the phrase, 'whatever the fact of its origin, envisages either two birds or two implements. From the double field of reference we may catch a hint that Hamlet sees in his schoolfellows [Rosencrantz and Guildenstern] both birds of prey and the king's tools.'

8 SEPTEMBER 1985

H OLY FOOL: someone with a good heart and not too sound a mind. That, roughly, summarised my thinking on holy fools until reading C. M. Woodhouse's observations on the Greek and English meanings of 'idiot' (see FALSE FRIENDS), which sent me to Dostoevsky's *The Idiot* and to the realisation of how hopelessly inadequate my 'definition' was. But where to find a better? No dictionary or encyclopaedia that I know has one, nor could I find any literature on the subject. Then a friend remembered a book, *Perfect Fools*, by John Saward (Oxford University Press, 1980). Here I learnt that 'it was St Paul who coined the phrase "fools for Christ's sake"' (1 Corinthians 4:10) so that he 'is therefore the original "doctor of folly"'.

'Holy folly', Mr Saward writes, sometimes expressed by

going about naked, living on discarded scraps of food, 'first emerges . . . among the founding fathers of Christian monasticism . . . in the early fourth century'. He has traced the movement to the present day, a new community of men and women. 'Mary's Followers of the Cross', 'living a most austere monastic life in the far west of Ireland, entirely in the spirit of . . . fools for Christ's sake.' The tradition has played an important role in Russian Orthodoxy and in Russian literature, supremely in *The Idiot*. The Russian word for holy fool is *yurodivy* 'the strange pilgrim', as the late E. H. Carr wrote in his book *Dostoevsky*, 'whose physical disabilities and mental derangement are the pledge of his holiness'. Dostoevsky's Prince Myshkin is one of the two great literary incarnations of the phenomenon (the other, from the opposite end of Europe, is Don Quixote).

30 MARCH 1986

HORRENDOUS is a word I find rather improbable, even comic – Chambers and the Concise Oxford label it 'colloquial' and Mrs Audrey Callaghan of Manchester wonders if it is a portmanteau word, from 'horrific' and 'tremendous'. It has been in the language for centuries – the first OED example, 'Your horrendous Sacriledges', is dated 1659 – but Mrs Callaghan puts her finger on its interesting aspect by associating it with 'tremendous'. Both come from Latin verbs, *horreo* and *tremo*, with the same meaning, to be frightened at, but very different origins. *Horreo* is 'akin to Sanscrit *hrish*' (Lewis and Short): first meaning, to stand erect, to bristle; *tremo* is translated from the Greek: first meaning, to tremble at (cf. 'tremulous').

20 OCTOBER 1985

HYPE: extravagant promotion of film, book etc. A useful word, but what is the origin? Unknown, say dictionaries, but another sense of 'hype' is stimulate: 'usually as hyped', says Volume II of A Supplement to the OED, 'as from the effects of a hypodermic [Greek *hypo-*, under, *derma*, skin] injection', so there is a possible source. I fancy another Greek prefix, *hyper-*,

over, in excess, as in 'hypercritical' or indeed 'hyperbole', exaggeration.

24 JUNE 1984

Mr Brian Gill of Edinburgh writes that while working for a record company in Toronto in 1961 he found that 'salesmen were instructed to "high-pressure" or "hipe" particular records to get them into the charts. As far as I can remember the verb was regularly used with this meaning and spelling in the trade press throughout North America.'

I NFER/IMPLY. 'Lucy directly drew her work table near her and seated herself with an alacrity and cheerfulness which seemed to infer that she could taste no greater delight than in making a fillagree basket for a spoilt child' – *Sense and Sensibility*. Mr Michael Paffard, of Keele in Staffordshire, writes apropos the quotation: 'In general it seems wise to try to take the heat out of disputes about usage, but I confess that confusions of "infer" and "imply" have always made me feel censorious. Can it be that Jane Austen knew no better, or was the surely useful distinction not established in her day?'

Webster's Ninth New Collegiate (1983) defines 'infer', 1: to derive as a conclusion from facts or premises ('We see smoke and infer fire'); 2: guess, surmise ('Your letter . . . allows me to infer that you are as well as ever'); 3a: to involve as a normal outcome of thought; b: to point out, indicate ('This doth infer the zeal I had to see him' – Shakespeare); 4: suggest ('Another survey infers that two-thirds of all computer installations are not paying for themselves'). A note states: 'Sir Thomas More is the first writer known to have used both "infer" and "imply" in their approved senses (1529).* He is also the first to have used "infer" in a sense close in meaning of "imply" (about 1530).** Both of these uses of "infer" co-existed without comment until sometime around the end of World War I. Since then, senses 3 and 4 of "infer" have been frequently condemned as an undesirable blurring of a useful distinction. Their use, especially with a personal subject, will still incur the wrath of some in spite of the usage of four centuries and the fact that the meaning will be clear from the context.'

Collins (1979) says such a sense of 'infer' is avoided by careful speakers and writers. The Longman Dictionary of the English Language notes that 'infer' has been used for 'imply' since the sixteenth century (*Great or Bright infers not Excellence –* John Milton) 'but today this usage is widely disliked. To avoid ambiguity it may be safer to provide either word with an adequate context (*I infer from your silence that you disagree*).'

6 OCTOBER 1985

*'Two such thinges as imply contradiction' (approved use of 'imply'); 'Whereupon is inferred al that the messenger wold haue fled fro by force' (approved use of 'infer'); both examples from *A Dialoge wherein he treatyd dyvers maters as of the veneration and worshyp of ymagys etc. (= A dialoge concerning heresys*).

**'The fyrste parte is not the proofe of the second, but rather contrarye wyse, the seconde inferreth well ye fyrst' ('infer' in sense close to 'imply'), from *A letter impugnynge the erroneous wryting of John Fryth against the blessed sacrament of the aultare*; all three examples quoted in OED.

On 13 July *The Sunday Times* reported that according to sources in Buckingham Palace the Queen was unhappy about Mrs Thatcher's approach to government. On 28 July *The Times* printed a letter from the Queen's Private Secretary, Sir William Heseltine, discussing the report and the issues it raised. Next day *The Times* printed a reply from the Editor of *The Sunday Times*, Mr Andrew Neil. It contained the sentence: 'At no time has *The Sunday Times* inferred that Her Majesty was party to or aware of any of the attitudes being attributed to her.'

Until reading that letter I had an open mind about the Webster Collegiate note, quoted above, that even when 'infer' is used in the sense of 'imply', the 'meaning will be clear from context'. I have changed my mind. Mr Neil has refuted Webster. I cannot tell in which sense he used 'infer'.

I NJUNCT. On 29 June David Leigh, reporting on the government's attempts to prevent *The Observer* publishing information – already revealed in Australia – from a former MI5 agent, wrote of a *Guardian* journalist who was 'about to be injuncted'. A reader asked me if Mr Leigh had invented the word 'injuncted'. I replied that the OED's earliest example of 'injunct', from an American newspaper, is dated 1887; the first English example is dated 1890. Volume II of A Supplement to the OED adds, 'Now in somewhat more general use'.

On 27 July Mr Leigh reported that *The Observer* and *Guardian* 'had both been injuncted'. On 3 August Sheriff G. H. Gordon, QC, of Glasgow, wrote in a letter: 'Now that *The Observer* has been injuncted by the High Court, are we to look forward to hearing that a new reporter has juncted the staff of the paper, or that there was a traffic jam where the M1 juncts the M6?' I was mildly amused but puzzled too. What should Mr Leigh have written instead? The letter's headline, which I had not noticed, enlightened me: 'Enjoined by law'. The Concise Oxford's fourth sense of 'enjoin', I found, is: 'prohibit by injunction'. Sheer ignorance on my part; I suspect many readers shared my ignorance.

A solicitor comforted me. '"Injunct" is perfectly correct; "enjoin" is archaic,' he declared roundly. A QC thinks 'injunct' is ugly – he prefers 'obtain an order restraining someone', which is five words. A young barrister also thinks 'injunct' is ugly and that 'a snooty Chancery judge might well ask, "Do you mean 'enjoin'?"' However, he uses 'injunct' freely in county courts.

Ugly or not, 'injunct', with its echo of 'injunction', is an expressive, economical, useful word.

7 SEPTEMBER 1986

Dumfries

DEAR SIR, *With regard to the apparent disquiet in English legal circles about the use of the word 'injunct' as a verb, why do they not overcome the problem by using the superior Scottish word 'interdict'?*

BRENDAN KEARNEY (SOLICITOR)

A few days after that column appeared I read in the *London Review of Books* of 4 September an article headlined: **26 July 1987, Court of Appeal: the Public Interest v. the Interested Public, Ex parte the Fourth Estate**. It was subtitled: 'Before Sir John Deodoran, Magus of the Scrolls, Lord Justice Clam and Lord Justice Null. Law Reporter: E. P. Thompson*.' It began: 'The Court of Appeal enforced circumlocutory injunctions restraining the Fourth Estate from publishing whatever any judge had injuncted, whether it had already been published or no. The greater part of submissions were heard in camera and the Court injuncted publication of the terms of the injunctions. Mr Janus Claws QC, for the Public Interest, regretted that formalities proscribed that any part of this hearing should be held in public. It was in the interest of the public that all information coming before it should be duly injuncted, but it was not in the public interest that the public should know.

'The mode of proceeding by injunction was a great convenience for the prompt administration of the Law. By registering the public interest before a judge in chambers, in the absence of the offenders to be injuncted, such offenders could be instantly silenced. If the offence continued, their assets could be seized and they could be imprisoned for contempt of court without the inconvenience and uncertainty of a trial . . . '

The piece ran to some three thousand words. At one point in his judgment the Magus of the Scrolls referred to an affidavit supporting the injunction. It had been submitted by an official named Sir Robert Strongarm, 'who held even higher office – that of Cabinet Usher' – than the 'tedious person now occupying Buckingham Palace', and in whom 'it had become accepted usage to vest the Royal Prerogative'. His office, indeed, 'like the Trinity, combined three persons into one, as Usher, as Head of All Services, and as Adviser on Security. When any enquiry into the public interest was involved, these three heads assumed their distinct functions and consulted each other. They then reassembled into the Awful Office of the Three-in-One, the Royal Prerogative made Flesh, and enunciated the Public Interest.'

His Lordship concluded: 'The question before the Court was

---

* Books by the historian and nuclear disarmer E. P. Thompson include *The Making of the English Working Class*.

not whether the public was interested in publication but whether the public interest could best be served by serving the interest of the public . . . What indeed was the public? It was a promiscuous rabble made up of numerous persons pursuing their own private interests . . . They were publicans all, and no doubt for the most part sinners. He would injunct the lot of them . . . The Court awarded costs against the Fourth Estate and confiscated all its assets. The offender was taken below in chains.'

INNOCENT/BENIGN. 'Princess Margaret has operation

on lung: Removed tissue "innocent", doctors reveal' – *Times* headline last month. That 'innocent' startled me – why not 'benign'? When a friend of mine had a brain tumour removed recently the word I hoped to hear (and, thank goodness, did hear) was 'benign'. To doctors both words merely mean opposed to 'malignant', or cancerous.

In general usage, 'innocent' is a far more powerful word than 'benign'. It is not immediately apparent why this is so. Etymologically it is a neutral word, deriving from the Latin *in-*, and *nocere*, to harm or hurt. 'Benign' comes from the more positive *benignus*, kind-hearted, kindly, friendly (of feelings); beneficent, liberal, bounteous (of action); fruitful, fertile, copious, rich (of things) – none of these seems to have much to do with tumours, innocent or not. Indeed, there is something absurd about describing a tumour as 'benign' – my friend certainly did not find hers particularly so before its removal. But if, to the layman, 'benign' seems not entirely suitable in this context, 'innocent' is a good deal less so; there is something holy about it. It always implies '"unacquainted with evil" (thus freq. of little children)' – OED. 'Child', as headline writers know, is a highly charged word. 'The Innocents' are 'the young children slain by Herod after the birth of Jesus, reckoned from early times as Christian martyrs'. Innocents' Day, 28 December, was formerly called Childermas.

10 FEBRUARY 1985

K EY. Mrs Joan Miles, of Cranbrook, in Kent, writes: 'My daughter, who teaches advanced English to Danish business-men in Copenhagen, asks if a new word is being used for telephone dialling, now that push-button phones are common.' Some years ago, when *The Observer* got a new telephone system, the operating manuals spoke of 'dial tone' and 'dialling a number' but, in references to the computerised facilities, we were told to 'key' the buttons. On receiving Mrs Miles's letter, I consulted Mrs Lesley Burnett, who is revising the Shorter Oxford. Her telephones too are now push-button and the manuals still refer to both 'dialling' and 'keying'. She thinks 'keying' is the obvious word and is looking into it. Meanwhile, things remain pleasantly confused. An example in the Oxford files reads: 'A mother left bound and gagged by robbers in her home dialled the police with her nose on a push-button telephone' – *Daily Telegraph*, 3 July 1980.

18 MAY 1986

L EISURELY. A reader is worried 'about the difficulty in obtaining adverbs from adjectives already ending in "-ly"'. She instances 'leisurely', as in 'he walked leisurely down the road' (which she has seen 'in quite high literary places'). But what should it be – 'leisurelily'? Again, what about 'ugly'? Surely one would not say, 'The cat walked uglily across the room'? I shared her dislike of 'leisurely' as an adverb and agreed about the ugliness of 'uglily' (even if I thought the example a contradiction in terms: for me a cat cannot move in an ugly manner). But whatever one thinks about the word, it is a perfectly good one, to be found in most desk dictionaries. The OED quotes from Philip Sidney's *Arcadia* (1586), which has 'trayling guttes' being 'ouglily displayed'. As for 'leisurely', judging from OED examples it is even older as an adverb (1486) than as an adjective (1604). The 1486 example is rather beautiful: 'Than softe and layserly fall oppon youre kneys', from *The Book of St Albans* (although I do not fully understand it, I like the book's full title too, *The bokys of haukyng and huntyng and also of cootarmuris . . . and the boke of blasyng of armys translayt and compylt at Seynt olbons*). Indeed, I like everything about 'leisure', its mere sound, its derivation (from the Late

63

Latin *licere*, to be permitted) and, of course, its meaning: 'The state of having time at one's own disposal; time which one can spend as one pleases; free or unoccupied time'.

The reader also asks, 'Why no antonym for "improve"?' I can think of 'mar' and 'worsen', but I have also found 'disimprove' in the OED. But it has quite fallen into disuse: the only desk dictionary I know that has it is Chambers. It appears in the two-volume Webster's Third New International (1961) but not in Webster's Dictionary of Synonyms.

22 APRIL 1984

Readers – and colleagues on *The Observer* – were quick to explain the old title of *The Book of St Albans*. I liked this version, from D. W. R. Whicker of Canford School: *The Books of Hawking and Hunting and also of Heraldry (Coats of Arms) . . . and the Book of Blazonry translated and compiled at Saint Albans.*

LEXICOGRAPHY. 'To make dictionaries is dull work',

Samuel Johnson says in his *Dictionary of the English Language*. Recently a two-day colloquium on lexicography was held in London under the auspices of the Fulbright Commission, a British–American foundation, to mark the bicentenary of Johnson's death and the centenary of the OED's first appearance. However much the participants – lexicographers, publishers, academics – might revere Johnson, they would not have agreed with him about dictionary-making. These people clearly relish their jobs. The whole thing was fascinating, if a bit technical: words such as 'lexeme', 'hyponomy', 'Labovian variable rule' were flying about.

Two practical points struck me. Dr Robert Ilson, an American teaching at University College, London (a dozen or so countries were represented; proceedings kept breaking into French), outlined variations in the way publishers presented their wares. Examples included: 'Almost 160,000 entries and 200,000 definitions' – Webster's New Collegiate; 'Over 40,000 headwords . . . 75,000 vocabulary items' – Concise Oxford; 'More than 180,000 definitions and references' – Reader's Digest Great Illustrated (he is its consultant editor). A little uniformity, he suggested, would be useful. Mrs Janet Whitcut of Longman spoke of the problem of ordering words with several senses. She strongly believed it should be by frequency, 'or at least the lexicographer's intuitive judgment of frequency if that is the best we can do, rather than historically. The "well" that is the opposite from "badly" should precede the one you draw water from.'

It was reassuring to find that even lords and ladies of lexicography can err. I heard the word *pace* (expressing polite disagreement) pronounced *pahchay*; the speaker's own dictionaries have *paysee* (as does the 'bible', Everyman's Pronouncing Dictionary). Another time there was some animated discussion of the 'lexicographer's art'. That was pitching it a bit high, I thought – no hint here of Dr Johnson's 'lexicographer, a harmless drudge' – but felt it was not my place to demur. Mr Patrick Hanks of Collins said firmly the word should be 'craft'.

4 NOVEMBER 1984

The proceedings of the colloquium have been collected under the title *Lexicography: An emerging international profession*, edited by Dr Ilson (Manchester University Press, 1986). The contributions are authoritative, packed with information – dense in the best sense of the word – and highly rewarding.

LINCH/LYNCH. Mrs J. Lilly of Solihull, in a letter, cites a recent *Observer* article that refers to someone as a 'lynchpin in the early nuclear programme' as an example of the growing confusion between the act of summary justice ('lynch') and part of a wheel ('linch'). Confusion, yes; I am not so sure about 'growing' – the confusion has been around for some time. A 'linchpin', which keeps a wheel in place on an axle, derives from 'pin' and Old English *lynis*, axle. 'Lynch', it is generally agreed, derives from an American of that name who, in the War of Independence, meted out summary justice to 'Tories', colonists who remained loyal to Great Britain. But who was Lynch?

The expression 'Lynch law', says the OED, 'is often asserted to have arisen from the proceedings of Charles Lynch [1736–97], a justice of the peace in Virginia, who in 1782 was indemnified by an Act of the Virginia Assembly for having illegally fined and imprisoned certain Tories in 1780'. (The entry, prepared for publication in 1903, shows 'Linch' as an alternative spelling, which suggests that the confusion goes back anything up to a couple of centuries.) Vol. II of A Supplement to the OED (1976) states magisterially that 'particulars supplied by Ellicott [in C. V. Mathews' *A. Ellicott*, 1908] clearly establish that the originator of Lynch law was Captain William Lynch (1742–1820), of Pittsylvania, in Virginia.' Most modern British dictionaries follow this. However, reputable modern American authorities, including *Britannica* and *Webster's Collegiate*, adhere to Charles Lynch; so does Collins. *Everyman's Encyclopaedia* says that 'the origin is variously ascribed to Colonel Lynch' (no Christian name given), 'who illegally whipped Tory conspirators, and to James Lynch FitzStevens, mayor of Galway, who, in 1493, tried his son for murder, and when prevented from publicly executing him, hanged him from the window of his own house.'

25 AUGUST 1985

M AJOR. Mr Martin Hatter of Bristol writes 'to make a few observations on the word "major". I'd always assumed that its correct use was to point out the greater of two or more things. Nowadays, though, it seems to be used as a sort of macho word for big. It's obsessively used on news bulletins – major investigation, major rescue operation etc., the most obviously memorable recent example being NASA Flight Control's speaking of "a major malfunction". But for over-using/misusing the word, Malcolm Bradbury should get some sort of award for his article on modern American literature in *The Observer* on 16 February. He speaks of major talents, major difficulties, three major periods, major writers, second major period, major moral crisis, major figures, major experimental novels, two major generations, major innovation, major new line, major names, major works and, finally, a major fictional tradition. Perhaps this is what one of the novelists Malcolm Bradbury writes of, Joseph Heller, was anticipating in *Catch 22* when he conceived of his ineffectual squadron commander, Major Major Major Major!'

The letter is salutary – I read the Bradbury piece with interest and, so accustomed am I to the word, without noticing the repetition. But I think Mr Hatter's view of the correct use of 'major' is a bit austere.

Even the OED entry, prepared for publication in 1904, notes that 'occasional uses (as "major poets") are suggested by antithesis with the recognised collocations of "minor".' Also, instead of 'macho word for big' I suggest 'useful alternative'. Imagine trying to write an introduction to a series of articles designed to capture the attention of readers without over-statement. Words like 'important', 'significant', 'outstanding' are at once boring and boastful. 'Major' is just right.

27 APRIL 1986

MALIGNANT.

Writing about 'innocent' (see entry) made me curious about 'malignant', not so much in its medical use of 'cancerous' as in general usage. The Latin word it derives from, *malignus*, means ungenerous, mean, grudging; (of soil conditions) unbountiful, niggardly; (of things) scanty, poor, small in extent; ill-disposed, spiteful, unkind, harmful –Oxford Latin Dictionary. Derogatory, certainly, but nothing like as fierce as 'malignant': 'passionately and relentlessly malevolent; aggressively malicious' – Webster's Collegiate. I wonder if it acquired this vehemence from its early association with ecclesiastical, then, in the seventeenth century, political conflict.

The first OED definition is 'disposed to rebel against God'. The designation 'church malignant', applied by the Fathers of the Church to followers of Antichrist, 'was also used by early Protestants against the Church of Rome'. Between 1641 and 1660 it was applied 'by the supporters of the Parliament and the Commonwealth to their adversaries'; an example refers to 'an unexpected reconciliation' that was 'most acceptable to all the Kingdome, except the malignant partie' led by Archbishop Laud and the Earl of Strafford. In 1642, the entry says, 'Charles I retorted the epithet upon the Parliamentary party': 'How I have been dealt with by a powerful malignant Party in this Kingdom, whose designs are no less than to destroy my person and Crown.' He lost that fight too: the Concise Oxford gives the historical sense of 'malignant' as 'supporter of Charles I against Parliament'.

It is very different in France. Synonyms of *malin*, the modern

67

French derivation, in the *Grand Larousse de la Langue Française*, include *astucieux* (astute), *débrouillard* (resourceful, especially at getting out of difficulties), *roué* (which, besides profligate, also means a cunning, sly, artful person). *'Il n'est pas très malin'* is paraphrased as *'Il ne brille pas par la finesse'*, 'He's not all that bright'. I feel that all this points to some subtle distinction between the English and the French, but I can't put my finger on it.

28 APRIL 1985

MAUNDY.

On Thursday, the Queen is due to make (or keep, or hold) her Royal Maundy at Ripon Cathedral, where she will distribute the Maundy money to 118 elderly people, one man and one woman for each year of her life. I shall be monitoring broadcasts of the ceremony: last year, I am reliably told, a newsreader in that bastion of the Queen's English, the BBC's World Service, pronounced it 'Maunday'. This is what linguists call folk etymology, the process by which an unfamiliar word is absorbed into the language by assimilating it to an existing word. 'Maunday' has been around since the 1500s, and though it has never succeeded in ousting 'Maundy' – as 'sparrow-grass' did 'asparagus' for about 200 years, until 'asparagus' began to make a comeback in the early nineteenth century – it persists.

'Maundy' comes from the Latin *mandatum*, injunction or commandment, and its first definition in the OED is 'the ceremony of washing the feet of a number of poor people, performed by royal or other eminent persons . . . on the Thursday before Easter, and commonly followed by the distribution of clothing, food or money'. It commemorates Christ's washing the feet of his disciples at the Last Supper and his injunction to them: 'A new commandment I give unto you (*Mandatum novum do vobis*), That ye love one another.' Maundy Thursday is also known as Sheer (clean) Thursday, from the ceremonial washing of altars on that day – Sir Thomas More's *The Answere to the Fyrste Parte of the Poysened booke* (1534) has a reference to 'The maundye of Chryste wyth hys apostles vpon shere thursday'.

On 4 April 1667 Pepys noted: 'My wife . . . had been to White Hall to the Maunday . . . but the King [Charles II] did not wash the poor people's feet himself, but the Bishop of

London did it for him.' One of the last monarchs to wash the feet of recipients, in 1698, was William III, who succeeded Charles's brother, James II (after James had fled the country in 1688). Some time after that, monarchs ceased to take part personally in the ceremony, until George V revived the old practice (without the feet-washing) in 1932.

31 MARCH 1985

MAY. Of all the months of the year May has by far the richest associations – OED references go on for page after page. There's May Day, of course, with its May Queen and the less familiar May King, or Lord: 'I . . . by all men chosen was Lord of the May' (Beaumont and Fletcher's *Knight of the Burning Pestle*). I did not know the expression 'Ill (or Evil) May-day: "the 1st of May, 1517, when the apprentices of London rose against the privileged foreigners, whose advantages in trade had occasioned great jealousy".' I look back fondly on May Week at Cambridge (so called, a don told me, 'because it is the first fortnight in June'), when the agonies of examinations are assuaged by May Bumps, May Balls and other jollities such as the Footlights show.

March has (or used to have) its strong March Ale, or Beer, but what is that compared with May-drink: 'white wine medicated with woodruff [low-growing herb with strongly sweet-scented leaves], drunk in Belgium and northern Germany'. Longfellow wrote: 'Fill me a goblet of May-drink, As aromatic as the May, From which it steals the breath away.' The German word it derives from, *Maitrank*, is obsolete, but not the drink, which is now known as *Maibowle* (*bowle* means bowl and is pronounced in the English way, but sounding the 'e').

6 MAY 1984

MAYORESS. Mrs Margaret Kyrle, of Chandler's Ford in Hampshire, writes apropos 'deaconess' (see entry): 'I am mayor of a borough (Eastleigh) and my problem is: how do I get people to call me "the Mayor", plain and simple? I am continually announced as "the lady Mayor" – there is no such office – or worse, "the Mayoress". People who ask are told that I like to be called "Madam Mayor" as opposed to "Mr Mayor", but still they feel the word is masculine and so needs a feminine suffix. Also, it is a pity that there is no generally accepted word for a woman mayor's husband. Mine has a badge proclaiming him "Mayor's escort", which has ambiguous connotations. The husband of another woman mayor in Hampshire is known as "Mayor's consort", which I don't like either. I am surprised', Mrs Kyrle adds, 'that there is still a problem of nomenclature, because there have been women mayors for many years.'

There have indeed. According to *Everyman's Encyclopaedia*, 'the first woman mayor ever elected in England' was Elizabeth Garrett Anderson (1836–1917), 'the pioneer of the movement to include women in the medical profession', who, in 1908, 'was elected mayor of Aldeburgh, her native town'. Dame Kathleen Ollerenshaw, Lord Mayor of Manchester 1975–6, has no doubt as to what the title should be. The opening words of *First Citizen*, her account of her year in office, are: 'Lord Mayor, you can relax now . . . ' and she still thinks that is the correct form of address. It's the office that matters, she says, not the sex of the holder.

In that useful book *Point of Order* (Shaw and Sons), Gladys Walker, JP, writes that although the status of civil heads is clearly laid down in two Acts (London Government 1963 and Local Government 1973), none of the many guidelines dealing with the Acts have directions on how to address women holding such office. No doubt as the effects of the Sex Discrimination Act become apparent, she says, 'the form of address . . . will be the feminine style, that is Madam Mayor'.

2 DECEMBER 1984

Members Room, Civic Centre
Ipswich

DEAR SIR, *Your discussion of the correct way to address a woman mayor leads to the question of how to address a woman councillor. 'Councilless' has, I think, never been tried and most local authorities seem to favour 'Councillor Mrs' or 'Councillor Miss'. To qualify the title in this way, however, does seem at best patronising and at worst offensive – imagine calling a woman doctor 'Doctor Mrs'. ('Doctress' had a brief vogue, I believe.) In Ipswich we are all now addressed simply as 'Councillor . . . ', which is just as natural as 'Doctor' or 'Inspector . . . ' etc.*

The late Edith Sitwell objected to being called a 'poetess' and I recently heard Penelope Keith say she was an 'actor'. For an entirely different reason we do not call a woman orchestra conductor a 'conductress' and the manager of the Ipswich Information Technology Centre refuses to be called a 'manageress', saying that this sounds as if she is in charge of a cake shop.

Yours faithfully

K. WILSON
Councillor, Ipswich Borough Council

Purley, Surrey

DEAR MR SILVERLIGHT, *In* Titles and Forms of Address – a guide to their correct use *(A. & C. Black, 1966), a passage reads: Mayors when ladies are addressed as 'Your Worship' or 'Mr Mayor'; colloquially 'Madam Mayor' is sometimes used, but this is not an established mode of address. On the Bench, 'Your Worship'.*

Yours sincerely
ERIC THOMAS

Mr Iain McDougall, a teacher in Coatbridge, Lanarkshire, and others take me to task for writing in the last paragraph of MAYORESS 'none of the . . . guidelines . . . have directions'. It should, they say, have been 'none . . . has'. Fowler's *Modern English Usage* (1926, repeated in the second edition, 1965) has: 'It is a mistake to suppose that the pronoun [none] is sing. only & must at all costs be followed by sing. verbs &c.; the OED explicitly states that pl. construction is commoner.'

MEDIATE.

'The basic assumption of the magazine *New York Review of Books* is that . . . politics is the crucial way by which reality is understood and mediated . . . ' – Radio 3 some months ago. I was startled, and went to my dictionaries, which confirmed that I was not wrong in thinking that 'mediate' indeed meant to try to reconcile disputants: most of them give something similar as the first definition. But the alternative definitions taught me that the sentence above does make sense. Collins – 'to serve as a medium for transferring (objects, information, etc)' – is typical. (The Concise Oxford gives that sense first; it does not appear at all in the Longman Dictionary of Contemporary Usage, which is aimed at foreign speakers of English.)

I suspect the usage encourages abuse – the Radio 3 quotation (from an otherwise admirable documentary) is woolly – but it is useful. The American Howard Nemerov has written:

> Here is Joe Blow the poet
> Sitting before the console of the giant instrument
> That mediates his spirit to the world

Oxford Book of Contemporary Verse

I would not presume to comment on those lines as poetry, but in the context 'mediate' looks just right to me. In an Open University talk on Radio 3 I heard that Christopher Wren used his draughtsmen 'to mediate between the master plan and mason and other workmen on the site'. His drawings were used 'to communicate to public and specialist alike'. Here too I find the use of 'mediate' unexceptionable.

21 OCTOBER 1984

MOGGY. Gavin Ewart (whose poem *A 14-year-old convalescent cat in the winter* expresses all that I have ever felt about cats in a lifetime of worshipping them; it begins, 'I want him to have another living summer' and ends by facing

> that last fated hateful journey to the vet
> from which there is no return (and age the reason),
> which must come soon – as I cannot forget)

writes: 'I have always considered "moggy" an insulting name for a cat. If I were a cat I wouldn't want to be called a moggy, it's like calling a black person a nigger. Or is it? I found nothing in Dr Johnson's great *Dictionary* (edition of 1765) and nothing in Webster (1875) but the OED gives it as "dial. . . . A pet-name for a calf or cow." It also gives "An untidily dressed woman." Partridge, besides "moggy . . . A cat: Cockneys (and dial.): late C.19–20", gives "mog. A cat: mainly schoolboys: C.20." He also has the "untidily dressed woman" (unconscious thoughts of old fur tippets?). Since the word began by denoting affection – the OED has a quotation about starving cattle, "poor moggies" – perhaps it's not as contemptuous as I thought.'

I too would like to know how the word came to apply to cats. (Incidentally, Mr Ewart's cat did not have another living summer.)

1 JULY 1984

Predictably my request for information on how 'moggy' came to be applied to cats provoked considerable response. C. H. Keeling of Guildford suggests that 'it is a corruption of "Margay" (*Felis wiedi*), a small and beautifully marked feline from South America, which a century and more ago was imported into this country in large numbers to keep down rats and mice in warehouses and factories'. Dr Humphry Greenwood of the Natural History Museum tells me he remembers from his days in the Navy hearing Catalina flying boats referred to as 'moggies'.

8 JULY 1984

MULTIPATERNITY? 'Britain and America are two
countries divided by a common language.' I had been trying for years to find the source of that saying when, in May, I read an item in the *Listener* on anti-American feeling in this country after the Libyan raid. The author, Joe Reid, wrote: 'A special relationship is still there, but the blood is feeling thinner these days. Dylan Thomas's smart remark about our common language looks now rather quaint and historical. Sadly, for the moment more than the language divides us.' I consulted Paul Ferris, author of Thomas's biography and editor of his *Letters*. After some thought, he remembered a BBC radio talk prepared by Thomas shortly before his death, in October 1953; it appeared in the *Listener* in April 1954 and was reprinted in *Quite Early One Morning* (Dent). In it Thomas spoke of the annual 'dazed and prejudiced procession' to America of European writers, scholars etc. 'confused and shocked by shameless profusion . . . and up against the barrier of a

common language'. So to Mr Reid, who recalled hearing the saying 'in a broadcast by Thomas in the fifties'. Could his recollection have been based on the quotation turned up by Paul Ferris? Quite possibly.

At this point a friend referred me to Hesketh Pearson's life of Oscar Wilde – several people had already suggested Wilde or Shaw but without precise references – and, sceptically, I leafed through it. Page 78 has: 'The English have really everything in common with the Americans except of course language' – dinner-party quip after Wilde's US tour. One more twist. In a World War II film with Anna Neagle shown last weekend on BBC2, an American officer observes: 'It only goes to show, like George Bernard Shaw says, there's nothing that divides nations like a common language.'

29 JUNE 1986

London W11

DEAR JOHN SILVERLIGHT, The origin of the 'two countries separated by a common language' quotation has come up a number of times on the Radio 4 programme Quote . . . Unquote *that I do, without my ever quite getting to the bottom of it. I had never heard Dylan Thomas mentioned in this context and I assume he was referring to what was already a well-known remark. It is possible to be a bit more precise with Wilde. The line 'We have really everything in common with America nowadays except, of course, language' appears in the* Canterville Ghost *(1887). Perhaps somebody else will turn up the Shaw reference so that we can date it, though I have a slight feeling that Wilde got there first. Just to be on the safe side I am putting both in my Dictionary of Twentieth Century Quotations due out next year.*

All good wishes

NIGEL REES

MUSHROOM. Another of those words that so irritate people by starting life as nouns and becoming verbs. Mr Derek Fane of Bognor Regis writes that he has come across it in Samuel Richardson's *Clarissa*: ' . . . the prosperous upstart, mushroom'd into rank'. The noun took on the sense of

'upstart' early: 'A nightgrowne mushrump, such a one as my Lord of Cornwall is' – Marlowe (1593). But unlike many nouns that became nouns almost simultaneously with their verbs, 'mushroom' took almost a century to do so, judging from the OED examples: *Clarissa* was published in 1747.

Mr Fane points out that the Richardson example appears to be unique – the OED describes it as a 'nonce-use'; certainly there are no more examples of the verb's use with social connotations. A century and a half later it appears in the sense of describing a rifle bullet's expanding and flattening: 'Such a bullet will mushroom on striking an animal', from *Travel and Adventure in South-East Africa*, by Frederick Courtenay Selous, big game hunter, traveller and natural historian – his name was preserved in the formation known as the Selous Scouts, who took part in the fighting that ended with the independence, in 1980, of Zimbabwe, formerly Southern Rhodesia. Next came the sense of 'to expand or increase rapidly' (Volume II of A Supplement to the OED): 'The flames had gone up to the very top of the house, and had then "mushroomed" out, as the firemen say' – New York *Sun*, 1903; 'The loosened soot of centuries came plunging in a mad cascade down the chimney; it met the floor with a soft and deadly violence and mushroomed up in a Stygian cloud' – *Busman's Holiday*, by Dorothy Sayers (1937), an eerie prefiguration of the image that has loomed over us ever since Hiroshima.

So to examples of the present dominant sense of the verb: 'A private Bill, promoted by the LCC, it is intended to secure greater control of the clubs which have mushroomed into existence in recent years' – *Daily Telegraph*, 1959; 'The number of publishing companies . . . which have prepared new editions of primary source [in linguistics] has mushroomed' – *Language*, XLVIII, 429.

18 MAY 1986

Musical Mysteries

MUSICAL MYSTERIES. The Latin *breve*, short, from which 'debrief' derives (see entry) is also English for a musical note that goes back to the thirteenth century – 'breve' because it was shorter than a 'long'. Later, to oversimplify, came the 'semibreve', white, oval-shaped, and nowadays the longest note normally used. Half its length is the 'minim', from *minima*, 'smallest', like a semibreve but with a tail; half that is a 'crotchet', black, also with a tail; half that is a 'quaver', with a hook on the tail.

'Quaver' makes onomatopoeic sense for the shortest note. 'Crotchet', diminutive of the French *croche*, hook, seems to make no sense at all. However, the crotchet was originally a minim, i.e. white, with a tail *and a hook*; later it became a black note without a hook. How 'crotchet' also came to mean 'whimsical fancy', says the OED, 'is obscure . . . Cotgrave [author of *A Dictionarie of the French and English Tongues*, 1611] appears to connect it with the musical note: "Crochue, a Quauer in Musicke, whence *Il a des crochues en teste* (we say) his head is full of crochets."'

The Germans, more logical, have *ganze Note*, whole note, for semibreve, half note (minim), quarter note (crotchet), eighth note (quaver), down to sixty-fourth note (hemidemisemiquaver). The Americans use these terms too, so in the film *Close Encounters of the Third Kind* I was surprised to hear the master of ceremonies order, 'Give her [the visiting space ship] six quavers.' The ship echoes the notes, then gives a new group. 'She gave us four quavers,' the technician reports. 'A group of five quavers. A group of four semiquavers.' A musicologist I know who has taught in the States says, 'Heaven knows what Americans make of it, but it's a great scene.'

29 SEPTEMBER 1985

MUTUAL.

Years ago I read in Fowler that the expression 'mutual friend' was a misuse of 'mutual'. However, 'common friend' is ambiguous and 'friend in common' sounds absurd, so, guiltily, I went on saying 'mutual friend'. My guilt has been purged. Sir Isaiah Berlin, in his enchanting *Personal Impressions*, writes of meeting Aldous Huxley 'in the house of a mutual friend': what is good enough for Dickens (*Our Mutual Friend*) and Sir Isaiah is good enough for me. Sir Ernest Gowers, editing Fowler, added: 'Perhaps it [mutual friend] should now be regarded as qualifying for admission to the "Sturdy indefensibles".' Perhaps Dr Robert Burchfield, who is editing the third edition of Fowler, will give it full blessing.

4 AUGUST 1985

DEAR MR SILVERLIGHT, *Another use of 'mutual' in the sense of common is to be found in Scotland. I enclose an item from the Edinburgh solicitors' property lists which describes a flat as being situated 'in a modern block in attractive mutual grounds'. This makes very odd reading at first sight.*

Yours sincerely

RALPH SIMMONDS

NO SURRENDER. Katharine Whitehorn wrote recently that Goetz, the name of the New Yorker who shot four black youths he thought were muggers, 'may pass into the language like Boycott or Bowdler or Lynch'. It passed into German two centuries ago. In Goethe's play *Goetz von Berlichingen*, set in the Peasants' War (1524–5), the imperial trumpeter summons Goetz to surrender. He replies: 'I have, as always, due respect for his Imperial Majesty. But as for your captain, tell him he can lick my arse.' That is the *Goetz Zitat*, the Goetz Quotation, and those who want to use it at less than full strength say: 'Goetz, act III, scene 4'. At Waterloo General de Cambronne, commanding the remnants of Napoleon's Old Guard, was credited with replying to a similar demand: '*La Garde meurt et ne se rend pas.*' It is generally agreed that what he actually said was '*Merde!*' Again there is a milder version: *le mot de Cambronne*. In December 1944 the US 101st Airborne Division was surrounded at Bastogne in the Germans' Ardennes counter-offensive. Called on to surrender, Brigadier-General McAuliffe, it is said, replied simply 'Nuts!' In an obituary the *New York Times* wrote: 'Unofficial versions strongly suggest that the actual language used by the feisty American general was considerably stronger and more profane than the comparatively mild "Nuts", but the official version will have to stand.'

Not a very grand defiance, but appropriate to the occasion.

17 MARCH 1985

ONTO.

Mr C. F. Scott, of Solihull, in Warwickshire, writes: 'Into, unto, upon – why not onto?' It's a word I have never been certain about, so I went to the OED to find that not only does it exist but is rather interesting. In Old English 'on' used to mean both 'upon', when it took the dative, and 'on' implying motion, when it took the accusative. Then case endings disappeared and ambiguity crept in. 'But', the entry goes on, 'while "in to, into" was in use by 900, the need for "on to, onto" appears not to have been felt before the sixteenth century, while its written recognition as a combination is still quite recent [entry ready for publication in 1903] and limited. Yet in the sense in which it corresponds to "into", "onto" is in speech a real compound, the "n" being shortened by its rapid passage into the allied mute "t", while in "on to" as two words, the "n" is long and does not glide into the "t".'

Recognition of 'onto' is still limited. Fowler, in a tetchy little article (carried unchanged by Sir Ernest Gowers in the 1965 revision), questions the need for 'onto' at all; the implication seems to be that 'on' will usually do by itself. The 'house style' of the Oxford University Press forbids its use and the Concise Oxford does not even give it a separate entry. Collins, however, notes that it 'is now generally accepted as a word in its own right'. About time too. In this OED example dated 1881, 'On a cliff there were men trying to send a rope out onto the ship,' I would not substitute either 'on' or 'on to'.

15 JULY 1984

ORCHESTRATE.

Mr Michael Gordon, of Chesham, Bucks, writes: '"Orchestrate", in the sense, say, "Picket violence has been orchestrated", nearly always has the undertone of the sneer about it. As someone who has been through the musical mill, I cannot help feeling that most of the people who confidently misuse "orchestrate" in this way would scarcely recognise the sound of an orchestra if they heard one.'

The source of the verb, 'orchestra', has an interesting history. The Greek *orchesthai* means to dance; *orchestêr* is a dancer; *orchestra* in the Attic theatre was the space on which the chorus danced, and this is the OED's first definition. The second is, 'part of the theatre . . . assigned to performers . . .

on musical instruments'; the third is 'the company of musicians themselves': 'But, hark! the full orchestra strike the strings' – John Gay, 1720. The first example of 'orchestrate', to arrange for an orchestra, is dated 1880; the figurative sense, to combine harmoniously, appeared about the same time. This has been still further extended: most modern dictionaries have something like 'combine so as to achieve maximum effect' (Chambers has 'best effect'). Both verb and noun can have pejorative connotations, as in Mr Gordon's example (I would describe them as 'sinister' rather than 'sneering'), but need not: 'A conference that collapsed because of poor orchestration was even worse than no conference at all' – *Time*, 17 October 1977 (from Vol. III of A Supplement to the OED).

23 JUNE 1985

O̶STRACISM. In his demanding but rewarding *Politics in the Ancient World* (Cambridge University Press) M. I. Finley writes that 'in an oft repeated story Plutarch tells how, on one occasion in Athens while the voting was under way for an ostracism, an illiterate rustic approached a man and asked him to inscribe his potsherd (*ostrakon*) for him with the name Aristides. The man asked what harm Aristides had done him. "None whatever. I don't even know the man, but I am fed up with hearing him called 'The Just' everywhere." Whereupon Aristides, for the man was he of course, duly entered his own name as requested.'

Sir Moses was using the story to make an historical point too subtle and learned to repeat in this limited space. What struck me was that word 'ostracism'. In a Greek lexicon I found *ostrakismos*: 'Banishment by potsherds to get rid of a citizen whose power was considered too great for the liberty of the state. Each person wrote on a potsherd the name of him who was to be banished.' A word I had been using unthinkingly took on a new, dramatic, concrete meaning. As with 'Aftermath' (see entry) the power of the metaphor was brought home to me.

5 AUGUST 1984

79

P ALLBEARER.

'The coffin was borne to the waiting hearse by six RAF pallbearers' – *Daily Telegraph*, 26 April. Mr Philip Bull, of Bevere Manor East, Worcester, asks apropos the quotation: 'Shouldn't the use of "pallbearer" be very rare, describing one of those (possibly equally distinguished) associates of a distinguished person who walk alongside the coffin, while it is borne on a bier or gun-carriage, as a relic of the days when a pall or canopy was held over the coffin?' Mr Bull is onto something. The OED has under 'pall': 'pall-bearer, -holder, -supporter, one of those attending the coffin, to hold up the corners and edges of the pall' (entry prepared for publication in 1904). The 1933 Concise is also uncompromising. Still retaining the hyphen – which has now been generally dropped – it has: 'person holding up corner of pall'.

Most modern dictionaries hedge their definitions with something like 'person who carries or escorts the coffin' (Collins). The change appears to have originated in America, to judge from the definition in the Longman Dictionary of Contemporary English (which is aimed primarily at non-native English speakers): '1, person who (a) walks beside a coffin at a funeral and (b) *now rare*, holds one corner of a pall; 2, AmE, a person who helps carry the coffin.' Here, then, is a word that has changed in sense remarkably without being noticed by most people (including me but not Mr Bull) or by dictionaries except for Longman, with the *'now rare'*. There is also the rather oblique Chambers definition, 'pall-bearer: one of the mourners at a funeral who used to hold up the pall'. Vol. III of A Supplement to the OED, unfortunately, has no 'pallbearer' entry, so the date of the change cannot be pin-pointed.

6 JULY 1986

P ANSIES.

After Solomon's Seal, the pansy has always been my favourite flower. Consider the derivation of its name: from French, says the OED, before 1500, 'a fanciful application of *pensée*'. Ophelia in her madness says: 'There's rosemary, that's for remembrance; pray, love, remember: and there is pansies, that's for thoughts.' 'Heart's-ease', one of the loveliest words in the language, is an alternative name for wild pansies; others are 'kiss-me-at-the-garden-gate', 'love-in-idleness', 'three-faces-

80

under-a-hood'. Oberon says to Puck,

> Yet mark'd I where the bolt of Cupid fell.
> It fell upon a little western flower,
> Before milk-white, now purple with love's wound,
> And maidens call it, Love-in-idleness.

So why is 'pansy' a term of abuse for homosexuals? Partridge
dates that use of the word from about 1925, of 'pansy-boy'
from about 1930. It quotes the *New Statesman and Nation* of
15 September 1934, in a piece about a Fascist meeting in Hyde
Park, as noting 'that there were, from the crowd, shouts of
"pansy-boys"', but gives no explanation.

From a great love to a great hate and another mystery. It
passes my understanding how 'weedy' came to mean 'weakly' –
'Grace . . . is looking rather pale and weedy' (Mrs Gaskell's
Wives and Daughters). After quoting Surtees, 'He rode a weedy
chestnut', Partridge has, 'Hence . . . lanky and anaemic . . . '.
I think of those words as I struggle in the garden to contain the
inexorable spread of ground elder and bindweed. I also try to
remember that a weed is only a 'wild herb growing where it is
not wanted' – Concise Oxford. Weeds are not completely
worthless. Cooked ground elder tastes rather like spinach.
Bindweed, a relative of honeysuckle, has itself pretty flowers.

1 JUNE 1986

P ASSION SUNDAY, I used to think, was just another
name for Palm Sunday, i.e. today. Dictionaries, I found,
disagreed. The OED, after giving the Latin source, *Dominica in
Passione*, has, 'The fifth Sunday in Lent [i.e. last Sunday];
reckoned as the beginning of Passiontide'; all my desk
dictionaries have something similar. However, under 'Passion
Sunday' *Britannica* has, 'see Palm Sunday', where one finds,
' . . . also called Passion Sunday, first day of Holy Week and
the Sunday before Easter, commemorating Jesus Christ's
triumphal entry into Jerusalem'. All rather confusing, especially
in view of another OED entry, 'Passion Week, the week
immediately before Easter . . . also (more recently) called Holy
Week'. The Concise Oxford doesn't help with 'Passion Week,
(1) week between Passion Sunday and Palm Sunday, (2) = Holy
Week'. Well, which is it? That is precisely what I want to

know, and here it is being left to me to decide.

The secretary of the Church of England's Liturgical Commission, Mr David Hebblethwaite, made all clear. Neither 'Passion Sunday' nor 'Palm Sunday' appears in the Book of Common Prayer, he said, but 'ever since the Middle Ages, there has been a strong tradition of calling the fifth Sunday in Lent "Passion Sunday"'. Then, in 1980, the Alternative Service Book appeared. In the Seasons section it has: 'Palm Sunday (1st before Easter)'. Palm Sunday has been made 'official'; 'officially', the fifth Sunday in Lent is, as it always has been, 'fifth Sunday in Lent'. Ten years earlier, the Roman Catholic Church began calling 'Palm Sunday' 'Passion Sunday' – in the Roman Missal it is *Dominica in Palmis de Passione Domini*.

So are the dictionaries all out of date? Yes, although the OED definition, prepared for publication in 1904, would have been in accord with popular Church usage of the time. Mr Hebblethwaite thinks that in such usage today the last fortnight of Lent is still widely known as 'Passiontide'.

23 MARCH 1986

---

23 March 1986 (i.e. Sixth in Lent)

The University College of Wales
Aberystwyth

DEAR MR SILVERLIGHT, In the Prayer Book proposed in 1928 (and rejected by the House of Commons) one reads: 'The Fifth Sunday in Lent, commonly called Passion Sunday' and, 'The Sunday Next Before Easter, commonly called Palm Sunday'. In the 'Order for the Celebration of the Holy Eucharist . . . ' authorised in 1966 by the Church in Wales [which was disestablished and disendowed in 1920 and became a separate, self-governing province – JS] *the terms 'Passion Sunday' and 'Palm Sunday' are used for last Sunday and today, respectively.*

Yours sincerely

EMYR TUDWAL JONES

PHILANDER.

PHILANDER. Professor F. R. Palmer, head of the Linguistic Science department of Reading University, asks apropos the rare use of 'misandry' (see SEX WAR): 'Why not consider the total absence of "philandry" (cf. "philogyny") – is it because of the semantically anomalous "philander"?'

'Philogyny' (love of women) is in a list of 'philo-' words in the OED and in three of my desk dictionaries. As Professor Palmer says, 'philandry' (love of men) appears nowhere, but rather than speculate on its non-appearance, I would rather consider 'philander'. It is indeed an odd word. The Greek *philandros* means (1) loving one's husband, (2) loving men, 'hence used as a proper name in story, drama, dialogue'. Its later use as a lover may result from its being misunderstood as meaning a loving man. A Beaumont and Fletcher play, *Laws of Candy*, has a Philander in love with Erota and, in a ballad, 'Phillis killed herself for loss of her Philander' (1682). The sense of lover is shown as obsolete. Another, current sense is 'a small wallaby, *Macropua brunii*, first described by Philander de Bruyn'.

The verb 'to philander' is 'to make love, esp. in trifling fashion' – OED entry prepared for publication in 1903, when 'to make love' still meant to court or woo. ('Didn't you make love to her?' Lord Augustus asks Lord Rufford in Trollope's *The American Senator*. 'No, my Lord, I don't think I ever did.' 'You don't think! You don't know whether you asked my daughter to marry you or not!') I don't know when it fell out of use in that sense, but nor do I remember ever hearing 'to make love' except as a euphemism for sexual intercourse. (The modern usage goes back a lot further in French. Under *'Amour (familiérement)'* the *Grand Larousse de la Langue Française* has: *'Faire l'amour, accomplir l'acte sexuel'* with an example from Trollope's close contemporary Théophile Gautier, *'Elle a vingt-six ans . . . Elle n'est plus ignorante, et n'est pas encore blasée. C'est un age charmant pour faire l'amour comme il faut, sans puérilité et sans libertinage.'*)

1 SEPTEMBER 1985

DEAR MR SILVERLIGHT, 'Making love' in the sense of flirting was in common use in the thirties and forties. I remember a Hollywood film of the classic period in which the heroine (it might have been Ginger Rogers), asked what she's been doing, replied, 'Making love in the park'. It caused a lot of hilarity when it was repeated on the TV during the past decade.

Sincerely

CAROL CLAXTON-VATTHAUER

Manchester

DEAR JOHN SILVERLIGHT, When I was in my early twenties, about 1950–1, I was acutely embarrassed to hear my mother referring to a couple 'making love', meaning 'courting', not the sex act.

Sincerely

(MRS) AUDREY J. CALLAGHAN

London N1

In the mid-1950s a very popular song, based on the old 'Tin Roof Blues', had 'Make love to me' and – whatever the hearer took it to mean – radio singers at any rate dared not imply more than the more innocent meaning. And what about the 1940 Make Love With a Guitar?

Best wishes

BILL MANLEY

POLICE/POLICY.

In 1813 Jane Austen wrote to her sister Cassandra: 'I am reading . . . an "Essay on the Military Police and Institutions of the British Empire" by Captain Paisley of the Engineers, a book which I protested against at first, but which upon trial I find delightfully written and highly entertaining.' A footnote in the Penguin Library Edition says: 'Though in the title it was "Military Policy", the OED shows that "police" was current in the sense of administration.' More than that: 'police' and 'policy', so different in sense nowadays, at one time were practically synonymous; so was 'polity'. All three derive ultimately from Greek *polis*, city or State, and all three had among early definitions the idea of an organised society.

'Polity' has hardly changed: the modern sense is 'political or governmental organisation', but no one I know has ever used the word. I seem to remember having heard or seen the expression 'polity of nations', but no dictionary bears out my recollection. The OED's first example of 'policy' in its 'chief living sense' – 'course of action adopted as advantageous' – is dated 1430. (It also used to have 'Scotch senses influenced by Latin *politus*, polished', e.g. ' . . . partly embellished park or demesne land lying around a country seat': 'Lord Breadalbane's seat and beautiful policy are too curious and extraordinary to be missed' (1775), Gilbert White's *Natural History of Selborne*.)

As the Jane Austen quotation shows, 'police' could still be found in its old sense in the early 1800s. But change was taking place. In 1830 Wellington wrote to Peel congratulating him on 'the entire success' of the Metropolitan Police. ('In early use', says the OED, the word 'police' commonly stressed the first syllable 'as often in Scotland and Ireland today'.)

8 JUNE 1985

Maidenhead

DEAR MR SILVERLIGHT, *The word 'policies' is still in use in Scotland in the sense of developed or planted land, even the most modest of back gardens. A chap I know in Dumfriesshire, when I visit him, always invites me to accompany him on an inspection of his policies, which are the tiniest of gardens, but impeccably maintained.*

Yours sincerely

HECTOR J. CORRIE

PS *My only recently late father always 'worked in his garden' but 'inspected his policies'.*

Apropos 'polity' and my remark that no one I knew had ever used the word, I learn from Sir Charles Gordon, former Clerk of the House of Commons, that in the essay he contributed to the collection *Parliament as an Export* (Allen and Unwin) he wrote, apropos one-party states in the Commonwealth, 'The role of parliament in these polities is, for the moment at any rate, subordinate to that of government.' And in his new book *The Siege* (Weidenfeld and Nicolson) Dr Conor Cruise O'Brien writes of the Palestinians' potential threat in Lebanon 'to the national polity'. I also said I had a recollection of reading or hearing the expression 'polity of nations' but that no dictionary bore this out. No wonder. As readers point out, I was mixing it up with 'comity of nations'. Other readers ask about 'policy' in insurance usage. It comes from the old French word *police* (1371), 'bill of lading, contract of insurance etc.' (OED), from the Greek *apodeixis*, a making known, demonstration, proof.

POPULIST.

In his *Observer* column of 8 June Alan Watkins wrote of the absurdity of the Cabinet's devoting half an hour to the hippie invasion of West Country farmland. However, he went on, 'Here was a good populist cause . . . Mrs Thatcher has lately taken up several similar causes, equally futile, facile and inexpensive, and almost as likely to pick up votes.' Mr H. Richardson, of Wonersh in Surrey, writes: '"Populist" seems to be one of *The Observer*'s favourite words, used in the sense of being popular.' However, 'my Concise Oxford Dictionary does not include this definition but refers to movements in certain countries towards public ownership. Is this another case of a word enlarging its scope following incorrect usage in the first place?'

The OED definition reads: 'An adherent of a political party formed in the US in 1892, the chief objects of which were public control of railways, limitation of private ownership of land . . . a graduated income tax etc.' Other demands were: free coinage of silver (the 'battle of the standards', gold v. silver, was one of the fiercest political controversies of the period); restricted immigration; the eight-hour day; prohibition of labour spies. Altogether, according to Samuel Eliot Morrison and Henry Steele Commager, in *The Growth of the American Republic*, the platform was looked on throughout the East – the Populists were strongly agricultural, based largely in the South and Middle West – 'as little short of communism, yet within a generation almost every one of the planks had been incorporated into law in whole or in part'. In 1896, says *Britannica*, the Populist Party was 'swept in with the Democratic Party'. The Democratic presidential candidate that year was William Jennings Bryan – 'You shall not crucify mankind upon a cross of gold' – and his defeat 'signalled the end of one of the most challenging protest movements in the United States since the end of the Civil War'.

So in 1907, when the OED's entry was prepared for publication, the definition was still relevant: the Populist Party, though in decline, was still fresh in people's minds. In 1982, when the latest Concise and Volume III of A Supplement to the OED appeared, it was purely historical. As a descendant of 'A New English Dictionary on Historical Principles' (as the OED was first entitled) the Concise quite properly gives the historical sense, as it does in, say, 'pylon': 'gateway, esp. of Egyptian temple'. But that sense is followed by, 'tall structure erected as support (esp. for electric-power cables)'; there is no counterpart for 'populist'. Volume III of A Supplement has a reference to the OED's sense 2, 'A member of the [nineteenth-century] Russian socio-political party advocating a form of collectivism', and has a sense 3: 'A member of a group of French novelists in the late 1920s and early 1930s who placed emphasis upon observation of and sympathy with ordinary people.' Sense 4 is, more generally, 'One who seems to represent the views of the mass of ordinary people.' One example seems to approach the word's modern sense – 'They are not Populists or Poujadists', *Listener*, 30 November 1961 – but otherwise it is all bland (so is every dictionary I know), ignoring the surely more usual pejorative sense of the word as used by Mr Watkins in his column.

In fact it has even more derogatory connotations. John Grigg, asked what the word suggested to him, replied: 'Demagogue'. That was also the word used by someone who has been observing MPs in the House of Commons for nearly forty years, although they agreed on second thoughts that that might be a bit strong. For a modern definition I suggest: vote-catching, without too many scruples about the causes espoused.

10 AUGUST 1986

Department of Slavonic Studies,
The Queen's University of Belfast

SIR, May I add to John Silverlight's valid explanation of the word 'populist' the fact that, as a historical term, it is especially associated with nineteenth-century Russia. It is the English rendering of narodnik, *a term applied to all the diverse groups and individuals who, between 1860 and 1900, propagated the aim of championing and guiding but also of learning from the 'people'* (narod) *– meaning, principally, the Russian peasants – by contrast with the Marxists, who pinned their faith to the far smaller though growing urban working class.*

Yours etc.

MARCUS WHEELER (PROFESSOR)

The London School of Economics and Political Science

DEAR MR SILVERLIGHT, *Your note on populism interested me. Fully to understand the concept, however, I think you need to go beyond linguistic dictionaries. In the* Fontana Dictionary of Modern Thought, *Professor Labedz, late of Stanford University, explains that populism originated among the Russian radical intellectuals in the 1860s. Labedz's definition is 'the promotion of political ends independently of existing parties and institutions by appealing to the people to exercise direct pressure on government'.*

Yours sincerely

HENRY PARRIS
Professor of Government

PORTMANTEAU: 'Large travelling bag that folds back flat from the middle' – Chambers. My interest in the word is prompted by a letter from Mr Allan Smith of Walsall, asking if there is a word for the amalgamation of two words into one. He cited 'servicentre' for garage 'and a word I coined myself for my pipework consultancy, "piperfect"'. (Mr Smith is a chartered engineer who advises on specialised pipe systems.) At first my

mind went blank. Then I remembered 'brunch': 'single meal instead of breakfast and lunch' – Concise Oxford, which added 'portmanteau word'. Of course. So to the OED and the discovery that the expression was 'originally applied by "L. Carroll" to a factitious word made up of the blended sounds of two distinct words and combining the meanings of both': 'Well, "slithy" means "lithe" and "slimy". . . . You see it's like a portmanteau – there are two meanings packed up into one word' – *Through the Looking Glass*.

Interesting. Even more so, from the usage point of view, is that while the Chambers definition is indeed the word's earliest sense (from *porte* and *manteau*; the modern French *portemanteau* means coat hanger), I cannot remember ever using it, or even hearing it used, which suggests that in that sense it is obsolescent, if not obsolete. Yet that is the definition given in all the dictionaries. That is to be expected in the Concise Oxford, based as it is 'on historical principles'. But what about Collins, which prides itself on giving priority to the 'most important *current* meaning' (my italics)? I suspect it is most frequently used nowadays (1) in the Lewis Carroll sense and (2) as a general description or category: 'The word "baroque" has come to be accepted as a convenient portmanteau term which covers the music composed between 1580 and 1750' – *The Times Literary Supplement*, 10 June 1949, quoted in Volume I of A Supplement to the OED.

16 JUNE 1984

Fowey, Cornwall

DEAR MR SILVERLIGHT, *When I first visited Australia in 1950 the question 'Where are your ports?' was often heard meaning, 'Where is your luggage?' Similarly, 'I must go and pack my port' meant 'I must go and pack my suitcase'. I recall hearing the word used in 1980 (my last visit to Australia). The Australians have always delighted in shortening words and 'port' is their version of 'portmanteau'. I have never heard them use it in full.*

Yours sincerely

PEGGY TURPIN

Mrs Rachel Minshall, of Mountain Ash, Mid-Glamorgan, was reminded of her time as a student teacher at 'a tiny infants school on the side of the mountain. One little girl constantly failed on the letter "b". At last I showed her the picture of a bag and said: "What is that, Gwladys?" She replied with almost a splutter: "Portmanteau". The emphasis in Welsh is always on the penultimate syllable, and how she pressed on it!' Kathleen Williams, of South Nutfield, in Surrey, writes that her favourite portmanteau word is 'insinuendo'. She adds, 'My own contribution to the genre is "bratinee", a children's matinee.'

Replying to my criticism of the Collins definition, Mr W. T. McLeod, managing editor of Collins English Dictionaries, points out gently (1) that the introduction explains that when *a* current sense (i.e. not the most important current sense) conveys the 'core' meaning, 'in that it illuminates the other senses', the 'core' may be placed first; and (2) that readers might like to know that the linguists' term for 'portmanteau word' is a 'blend'.

PRIVATE: 'Of a conversation, communication etc.: Intended only for or confined to the person or persons directly concerned; confidential' – OED. Last winter the National Westminster Bank sent me – and some five million other customers – a leaflet explaining a new system of bank charges. Since it is a joint account, and the only occupants of the house are my wife and myself, I wondered why the envelope was marked 'Private'. Who did they think might open it without authority? A visitor? My wife wondered why a letter relating to a joint account was sent to 'J. A. Silverlight Esq.' Then I remembered receiving at *The Observer* a NatWest letter addressed 'Features Editor', also marked 'Private', telling us about a thoroughly worthy scheme devised by the bank to involve schoolchildren with 'social needs in their locality'. Did they really want us to treat the matter as private? Our Business Section recently had a press release marked 'Private *and Confidential*' (my italics) from a firm dealing with computer staff. I have just thrown in the waste-paper basket a similarly marked missive addressed 'The Editor'. It's a fairly safe bet that all such letters sent to us will indeed be kept private. We won't print a word.

20 MAY 1984

90

PROFESSION.

The subtitle of Professor John Kenyon's excellent and highly readable *The History Men* (Weidenfeld and Nicolson) is 'The Historical Profession in England since the Renaissance'. I found the notion novel, but then I have mixed, not to say confused, feelings about the word 'profession', especially in relation to my own craft. The OED's first definition is 'The action . . . of professing', which is the sense of ' . . . all who profess and call themselves Christians' (Book of Common Prayer) or 'Mr Hutton, of the Moravian profession' (Boswell's *Dr Johnson*). Later comes: 'A vocation in which a professed knowledge of some department of learning or science' is applied 'to the affairs of others . . . specifically divinity, law, and medicine; also the military profession. In wider sense any calling by which a person habitually earns his living.' At this point the lexicographer (the great James Murray himself) noted, 'Now [entry prepared for publication in 1908] usually applied to an occupation considered socially superior to a trade . . . but formerly, and still in vulgar (or humorous) use including these.' Among 'these' are: 'Their profession is to robbe and steal from their neighbours and to make them slaues' (1600) and 'The Professions of these persons, so vnfortunately drowned, were: – 1, a Haberdasher; 2, a Taylor; 3, a Saddler; 4, a Barber; 5, a Waterman' (1616).

My view (not original) of a profession is: a vocation whose followers lay down the qualifications for entry into it and themselves (or their delegates) can expel someone found guilty of professional misconduct. That is too narrow, I know: usage is against me – D. Watkins, in our Letters Page last Sunday, paying tribute to Edward Crankshaw, wrote that his death was a severe loss to the professions of historiography and journalism. I agree wholeheartedly, but I still cannot rid myself of my notion about the word (which doesn't prevent me from using 'professional' when I wish to compliment a fellow journalist).

16 DECEMBER 1984

Two professional people have written apropos 'profession'. Someone signing him- (or her-) self 'A. Pothecary', of Hendon, North London, sends a cutting from the *Pharmaceutical Journal* of 15 December naming six members of the Pharmaceutical Society as Fellows of the Society, five for distinction in the *profession* of pharmacy, one for distinction in the *science* of pharmacy (my italics). I asked the Society to explain the difference. 'Science', I was told, referred to work in academia or in industrial research, 'profession' to the practice of pharmacy in the community, including hospitals; one of the five was a journalist. And the Rev Clifford Warren, of Machen in Gwent, looking at 'profession' from the social (one might even say idealistic) point of view, commends this quotation from a book, *The Protestant Ministry*, by his fellow cleric Daniel Jenkins: 'A professional man is one who, in the judgment of his peers has proved himself competent in the exercise of the work he has undertaken. He is one who is not limited in the performance of his duties by a timetable or, when he understands his work aright, by the ability of those he serves to pay him. He does not practise his skill as a mere technician, but as a human being conscious of the fact that he is dealing with human beings in the complexity of human situations.'

17 FEBRUARY 1985

Tividale, West Midlands

DEAR MR SILVERLIGHT, *The distinction drawn by the* Pharmaceutical Journal *in connection with professions has parallels elsewhere. Our taxation schedules preserve the distinction between tradespeople and those conducting professions or vocations. All self-employed persons in these categories are taxed under Schedule D – you probably are – but the Income and Corporation Taxes Act 1970 specifies that Schedule D shall charge under its different cases: 'Case I – tax in respect of any trade carried on in the United Kingdom or elsewhere. Case II – tax in respect of any profession or vocation . . . '*

The origin of the distinction is obscure, probably from amalgamations of various preceding legislative attempts to enhance the Exchequer's revenue. Its object is obscure too: it confers no advantage on either professional or tradespeople. When, while undergoing training, I asked why it was there, I was told, 'Because it's always been there.'

Yours sincerely

W. M. JOHNSON
H. M. Inspector of Taxes, Birmingham 6 District

RACK/WRACK.

Mr Len Atkinson, of Shipley in Yorkshire, has sent in an *Observer* cutting in which Israel is described as 'wracked by the world's highest inflation rate'. The noun 'wrack', seaweed that has been cast ashore, is akin to 'wreck'; the verb 'to wrack', to drive to destruction, is archaic. The word in the cutting should have been 'racked', an extended use of 'to rack', to torture by stretching the joints of a person on the rack – 'let him pass', says Kent in that intolerably poignant last scene of *King Lear*, 'he hates him/That would upon the rack of this tough world/Stretch him out longer.'

The intrusive 'w' is a common error – literate people often write of someone being 'wracked with pain' – and a persistent one: the earliest OED example of the 'erron.' use of 'wrack' dates from the 1500s. The confusion extends even to dictionaries. Take the phrase 'rack and ruin'. Logically it should be 'wrack, etc.', but most dictionaries have 'rack, etc.', with 'wrack, etc.' as an alternative; Collins has both, with no indication as to preference.

11 NOVEMBER 1984

Eric Baird, of Greystones, County Wicklow, writes that it may have been an error to describe Israel as being 'wracked by inflation' but whoever did so 'is in good company. Your quotation from *King Lear* in the First Folio has "wracke", and this is probably what W. S. wrote. Anyway, I think "wracke" looks better and may just possibly sound better.'

Mr Baird has a point; I should have checked. But I still prefer 'rack', not so much because it is 'correct' but because it graphically evokes the image of the instrument of torture that gave rise to the extended use of the word.

25 NOVEMBER 1984

RATE-CAPPING.

How did the Rates Bill, which goes to the Lords next month, become known as the rate-capping Bill? Mr C. R. K. Perkins, of Leckhampton in Gloucestershire, asks: 'Is it too fanciful to suggest that "rate-capping" is a journalistic off-shoot of "knee-capping"? Are we to infer that critics of central government view the action to deprive spendthrift councils of rate support grants as analogous for the actions of terrorists who maim their victims?'

An interesting thought, but the sense that occurs to me is that of capping an oil well. But who coined it? Not the Department of Environment, which blames the Press. 'We fought shy of it,' an information officer says, 'we preferred to call it "limiting".' The earliest example I have found in print is in *The Times* on 2 August. In his report outlining the proposals in the White Paper, David Walker, then the paper's Local Government Correspondent, included a table headlined CANDIDATES FOR RATE CAPPING, listing 13 local authorities. Mr Walker neither claims nor disclaims credit for inventing the expression. He thinks it more likely that he heard it in one of many anticipatory discussions on the measure. Whatever the origin, it is a vivid metaphor, with its implication of sharply bringing something under control; the only dictionary I know that specifically defines 'cap' in the sense of capping an oil well is the two-volume Webster's Third New International. (See CAPPING.)

Incidentally, talking of the Lords, when is some feminist group going to denounce using the word in that sense as sexist, ignoring as it does the Upper House's 46 women life peers and 18 hereditary countesses and baronesses in their own right? If it ever becomes a problem (somehow I doubt if it will) there is an easy way out: House of Peers. It does not occur only in *Iolanthe*. When Black Rod summons the Commons to hear the Queen's speech at the Opening of Parliament he says: 'The Queen commands this honourable House to attend Her Majesty immediately in the House of Peers.'

25 MARCH 1984

R EFUTE. 'The police today refute the idea that . . . ' – report in *The Observer*; 'I wish to refute here and now the underlying inference that . . . ' – Deputy Chief Constable of Greater Manchester, quoted in the *Guardian*. Some years ago I quoted Dr Robert Burchfield of the Oxford English Dictionaries as fearing that the distinction between 'refute' and 'deny' would become even more blurred than it already is, in the next decade or so. Those two recent examples, with many others, bear him out. Indeed I have noted only one instance in the past few months of what I consider the correct use of 'refute' – by Dr Conor Cruise O'Brien, in a *Listener* review of a new edition of Yeats's letters. Commenting on the blurb's claim that 'without exception' the letters were vividly entertaining, he writes that the claim 'could easily be refuted by an abundance of tedious quotation'. To refute is to disprove, not to argue with, deny, reject or even to rebut.

Dr Ian R. Haldane, of St Andrews in Fife, writes: 'To use "refute" instead of "deny" is far more misleading than is immediately apparent: it confers on the speaker a quite unwarranted authority to pass judgment in his own case. It is perhaps the prime "weasel word" of our day.' I agree, although I fear that like 'deprecate/depreciate' (see entry) 'refute' is a losing if not a lost cause. But Dr Haldane has allies. A letter in the *Guardian* of 1 April reads: 'The Deputy Chief Constable of Greater Manchester has certainly denied and rejected the allegations about harassment of students, but he has not refuted them. The public would be very interested to see him do just that – if he can.' It is signed, 'Jeanne Forster, (Prof.) Leonard Forster, Cambridge.'

11 MAY 1986

RUBBISH. Mr David T. Roberts of Bristol writes that he has become 'increasingly aware of the word "rubbish" being used as a verb'. In particular he cites last year's report by the Church of England Commission, *Faith in the Cities*, 'which has been greeted with disdain by certain members of the government. Their attitude has been described by other politicians as having "rubbished" the report.'

Here is another example of a process that, as I wrote in TRYST (see entry), goes back at least a thousand years. 'To rubbish', to critise severely, is not as old as that, but it has been around some time – Volume III of A Supplement to the OED describes it as 'orig. and chiefly Austral. and NZ'; the earliest example is: 'if Verity was going to tramp you for burning the tucker . . . he would have rubbished you long before this' – A. G. Hungerford, *Riverslake*, 1953. The first British example is: 'This live show had a live and participating audience; so Hockney got briefly rubbished the moment his film ended' – *Guardian*, 16 October 1972. On 12 January 1975 *The Observer* had, 'His plight, and that of the cricketers, have both been latched onto as a chance, not to be missed, of rubbishing the Poms.'

Two examples of verb-making that even I, for all my permissiveness, find hard to stomach (which verb, incidentally, goes back in that sense at least to the 1670s) are: ' . . . power has worked to marginalise women' – from a book reviewed in the *Listener* of 30 January 1986; 'What has particularly incensed and increduled MPs . . . ' – *Daily Telegraph*, 19 July 1985. In contrast consider the verb 'to pleasure'. I once heard Sarah, Duchess of Marlborough, quoted as saying or writing: 'M'lord home from the wars and did pleasure me thrice without removing his top boots.' I cannot, alas, document that, but Volume III of A Supplement has: 'Silvius doth shew the citty dames brave sights, And they for that doe pleasure him a nightes', 1616. (The ancient Greeks had the verb *charizomai*, to pleasure, but to them the pleasurer was always a man; the pleasured could be of either sex.)

Which brings us to the phrase I quoted in TRYST: 'do the naughties practically on camera'. This sense of 'naughty', like 'to rubbish', also comes from 'Austral. and NZ'. Volume II of A Supplement quotes *The Times Literary Supplement* of 12 October 1962: 'Would you please whisper in the ear of the young lady who reviewed *The Stuart Case* in your issue of August 10 that "to have naughty" . . . is throughout the South Seas the polite and strict analogue of "to have sexual intercourse". Another example reads: 'I smiled, remembering his oft-repeated remark: "I get a lot of knock backs but I get a lot of naughties"' – F. Hardy, *Legends from Benson's Valley* (1963). There is also the verb 'to naughty', with the same sense.

9 MARCH 1986

Sardonic

SARDONIC. Mr K. Sedgwick, of Dublin, writing apropos the derivation of 'ostracism' (see entry), points out that 'sardonic' comes from the Greek name for a plant from Sardinia 'which was said to screw up the face of the eater'. Worse than that, says the OED: the ancients thought it produced 'facial convulsions resembling horrible laughter, usually followed by death'. And according to an example dated 1794, 'Homer first, and others after him, call laughter, which

conceals some noxious design, Sardonian', another form of
'sardonic'. Odysseus laughs sardonically at one of the suitors.

21 OCTOBER 1984

Winster, Derbyshire

DEAR MR SILVERLIGHT, *May I draw your attention to the medical
phrase 'risus sardonicus'. As in ancient usage it conveys description of spasm of the muscles of the mouth, giving rise to a
'sardonic smile' which is present in the latter stages of strychnine
poisoning and tetanus; hence, in the past, a close precursor of
death.*

Yours sincerely

(DR) D. L. L. JAMES

SEAFOOD. 'Considering their relatively low position on the
evolutionary ladder,' writes my lexicographer friend John
Ayto, 'molluscs and crustaceans have contributed a surprising
amount to the language. An amusingly puny person is a
shrimp. Limpets are proverbial for their adhesiveness. To
Pistol, in the *The Merry Wives of Windsor*, "the world's 'mine
oyster'". An oyster is also an uncommunicative person –
J. B. Priestley, in *Angel Pavement*, has: "I never knew anyone so
close, you old oyster, you!" In Australia to "come the raw
prawn" is to try to deceive someone. Closely guarded secrets
have to be winkled out. "Lobster" used to be a contemptuous
term for a British soldier; originally it was applied to a regiment
of Roundhead cuirassiers; later the reference was to the
soldiers' red coats. The crab has had a particularly rough deal,
being taken as the archetype of grouchiness, because, says the
OED, of its "crooked and wayward gait", and the "contradictory
and fractious disposition which this expresses".'
    'To catch a crab' is 'to make a faulty stroke in rowing
whereby the oar becomes jammed under water' and the handle
can be driven against the rower's body 'with sufficient force (if
the boat be in rapid motion) to force him back out of his seat
and to endanger the capsizing of the boat' (OED). There is the
crab louse. There is the Crab constellation and the Crab as the

fourth sign of the Zodiac, both commonly known as Cancer. Some astrology columns have discarded this dread word and instead use 'Moon children', which is what they call people who are born under the sign of Cancer: in astrology the Moon is closely associated with this sign.

27 OCTOBER 1985

S̲ERIOUS.

Shortly before he was killed by Bulgarian fascists in 1944, Major Frank Thompson, RA, aged 23, wrote to his younger brother Edward, the historian and nuclear disarmer: 'I have a letter from Greek Maroula, in which she exhorts me to be serious . . . Serious is not a good translation for the word, which corresponds to the French *sérieux*. That is a far deeper and more comprehensive word, expressing an attitude to life not incompatible with lightheartedness' (from *There is a Spirit in Europe*, a memoir of his brother by Mr Thompson).

A small matter, perhaps, but it is in keeping with Frank Thompson's remarkable personality – 40 years after he was put to death distinguished contemporaries still talk about him with affection and respect – that he should have had that insight into the deeper meaning of 'serious'. It was not generally considered a compliment then. I'm a contemporary too and I hated being told, especially by girlfriends, 'Oh, don't be so serious.' Nowadays serious is what everyone wants to be – professionally it is the highest tribute I can pay someone. Conversely the biggest put-down I know is 'not serious' – it sounds even worse in French: '*un homme pas sérieux*'. A very senior churchman who approves of the ordination of women 'but not yet' explains his temporary opposition by saying that he wants it to be seen by the Roman Catholics and the Orthodox 'that the Church of England is taking the problem seriously'.

The current word of disapproval in that context is 'solemn', I don't know why. Perhaps it is because people are nervous about the word's ecclesiastical assocations: the first OED definition is ' . . . having a religious character; sacred'. The Greek word Frank Thompson's Maroula would have used is *sovarós*, not *semnós*, solemn, which, as in English, can have unflattering as well as religious connotations.

9 DECEMBER 1984

E. R. Evans, of Bradford-on-Avon, Wiltshire, writes: 'Some years ago a radio broadcast brought home to one the special significance which the French give to the word. A travel broadcaster was describing the visit of a group of tourists to some Greek ruins. The guide explained that a certain huge carving was in fact a phallic symbol. Nobody spoke, until a Frenchman murmured, awestruck, *"Mon dieu, c'est sérieux, ça!"'*

17 FEBRUARY 1985

SEX WAR. Mr William Moodie of Edinburgh and Mrs
Kathleen O'Malley, a teacher at Our Lady and St Chad Comprehensive, Wolverhampton, ask: What is the female equivalent of misogyny? I consulted Mrs Lesley Burnett, of the Oxford Dictionaries. 'Look at Vol. II of A Supplement to the OED,' she said. There it was: 'misandry, hatred of males', from Greek *misos*, hatred, and *andros*, of a man – not *anthropos*, which means mankind. The one example was from an article on *Much Ado About Nothing* in the spring 1946 issue of F. R. Leavis's *Scrutiny*: 'In the absence of precedents, she [Beatrice] could do no better than she does do, follow masculine example and answer to their affected misogyny with the affectation of misandry.'

Using Oxford's computer links with American data bases, Mrs Burnett found that in 1983 the columnist William Safire referred in the *New York Times* to the appearance of 'misandry' in the third edition (1961) of Webster's Third New International. A Longman lexicographer I consulted, Mr Brian O'Kill, found it in the second edition (1934) of Webster's – and in *Larousse de la Langue Française* he found *misandre*, dated 1920. Back to Mrs Burnett, who found an earlier appearance in the 1909 Supplement to the (American) Century Dictionary.

Every dictionary I know has 'misogyny'. Of my desk dictionaries only two, the latest Chambers (1983) and the Reader's Digest Great Illustrated (1984), have 'misandry'. It is interesting, too, that 'misandry' was coined so much later than its counterpart. The OED's first example with 'misogynist' is: 'Swetnam's name, Will be more terrible in womens eares, Than euer yet Misogynists hath beene', from *Swetnam the woman-hater arraigned*, published in 1620 in reply to Joseph Swetnam's

The arraignment of lewd, froward and unconstant women. Does all this suggest that women on the whole, very sensibly, have not felt a need for a female equivalent? (See PHILANDER.)

9 JUNE 1985

SHALL/WILL.

In WHO/WHOM (see entry) I quoted Professor John Honey of Leicester Polytechnic as foreseeing 'a time when we will abandon differences of pronoun case'. Dr Donald Dawes of the Polytechnic of North London asks if Professor Honey thinks that the distinction between 'shall' and 'will' is also disappearing. I put the question to him. Yes, he replied. What he describes as Honey's Law, which he quotes to foreign audiences when explaining how he thinks English is evolving, states: 'If in doubt, always use "will".' He himself, he says, was taught in the 1940s the conventional paradigm: 'shall' in the first person, singular and plural, 'will' for the rest, except when something more than 'simple futurity' is involved, e.g. emphasis and prediction. Now, however, he contends that 'will' is usable in *all* cases. As a striking example of Honey's Law he quotes the Church of England's Alternative Service Book (1980). The Creed's 'And he shall come again with glory . . . ' is now 'He will come again . . . '

So is the 'correct' use of 'shall' and 'will', the non-observance of which, says the OED, 'is the mark of Scottish, Irish, provincial or extra-British idiom', doomed? It seems so: 'The nice but complex distinction between "shall" and "will" is dying; let it die,' Philip Howard writes in his *State of the Language*, which has just come out in paperback (Penguin). His tone is regretful and, 'extra-British' that I am (born in Canada, brought up in the States), I share the regret. An excellent note in Longman's Dictionary of the English Language agrees that the distinction is dying, but adds: ' . . . a useful distinction can still be made between "*shall* you join us" (= are you going to) and "*will* you join us" (= please do)'.

25 MAY 1986

DEAR MR SILVERLIGHT, *The version of the Creed in the Alternative Service Book 'He will come again' may well agree with Honey's Law but is inferior to the original 'He shall come again' on two grounds. 'He shall come again' contains an element of promise – God's promise about His son – that is lacking in 'He will'; and as a matter of euphony 'He will' sounds very feeble compared with 'He shall'.*

Yours sincerely

FRANCIS JONES

Most people who have commented on my gloomy prognosis for the distinction between 'shall' and 'will' quote the classic example of the man who fell into the river and instead of shouting, 'I shall drown and no one will save me!' (simple future) shouted, 'I will drown and no one shall save me!' (determination), so that he duly drowned. However, the little cautionary tale does not simply illustrate the perils of faulty usage. It is also an example of what the OED describes as a 'mark of Scottish, Irish, provincial or extra-British idiom'. The point was made by Mr Alfred Griswell of Worcester, whose victim was 'a Frenchman', and by Dr S. O. Lucas, of Hemel Hempstead in Hertfordshire, who remembers his father, the scholar, critic and poet F. L. Lucas, as telling the story about 'a Scotsman'. (A. E. Housman may not be a poet of the first rank but no one's verse has given me greater pleasure. I discovered him thanks to an essay, *Few but Roses*, in one of the books by F. L. Lucas which were a delight to me at school. At Cambridge, after the Second World War, it was again a delight to attend his perceptive, authoritative lectures.)

Mr Patrick Gribben of the Studio School of English, Cambridge, referred me to *The English Verb: An Exploration of Structure and Meaning* by Michael Lewis (Language Teaching Publications, Hove) which claims that there is 'a general, easy-to-understand difference' between the two words. It contrasts the questions 'What time will we arrive?' and 'What time shall we arrive?' The first 'invites the listener's opinion of what, given the present circumstances, is inevitable. The question would be appropriate during a journey from a passenger to the driver: "You know the circumstances, please give me the information." With "shall", the listener is involved in the creation of the inevitability. The question suggests, "What time do you think it is appropriate for us to arrive?"' Mr Gribben agrees and adds, 'So the distinction will survive.' We'll see. Interestingly, although the Alternative Service Book has 'He will come again' in the Creed instead of 'He shall . . . ', it has retained 'shall' in the Commandments: 'You shall have no other gods but me.'

20 JULY 1986

London NW3

DEAR JOHN SILVERLIGHT, Has this point been put forward yet? The use of 'shall' carries unmistakable overtones of threat, e.g. 'You shall go back to school, Edith' (with 'and no nonsense either' as an implied extension). The use of 'will' carries no such overtones, even when the verb is unstressed, e.g. 'You will go back to school, Edith' (with a 'won't you?' the likely follow-on. Or if unstressed, with an informative 'at the end of the month').

Similarly in the negative: 'You shan't go to Betty's party' is a firm directive, whereas 'You won't go to Betty's party' suggests an innocuous 'will you?' follow-on, or perhaps 'I suppose'. The above distinction may be on the way out – along with the exercise of parental discipline – but I fancy that, if moribund, it is by no means yet quite dead.

Yours truly

MAX CHAPMAN

S‎LEAZE.

Simon Hoggart, reporting from Washington last month that a former aide of Mr Reagan was accused of using his influence with the President to earn huge sums of money 'in a manner which is definitely dubious', wrote: 'Deaver has always denied any wrong-doing, though there is a term here for this not-quite-crookery: "sleaze".' The 'sleaze factor', Mr Hoggart tells me, is common usage in Washington.

The noun was new to me and I thought it most apt.

Volume IV of A Supplement to the OED, which came out last month (crowning the daunting task Dr Robert Burchfield and colleagues took on 29 years ago), has: 'Sleaze (slang, back-formation from "sleazy"): squalor, sordidness . . . ' The first example, from the *Listener*, is dated 1967. The word does not appear in any of my British desk dictionaries or the 1977 *Webster's New Collegiate*. (Another sense in Vol. IV is 'person of low moral standards'. One of the examples, from *Time*, reads: 'Oh God, red nail polish – I look like a sleaze.' There is also '"sleazo", US slang, something sleazy, something porno-graphic', with the example 'Norman Maller said he liked sex movies, especially "love pornies" and "the sleazos"' – *Brisbane Courier*, 4 January 1978.)

'Sleazy', nowadays about as derogatory a word as I can think of – 'disreputable', 'sordid', 'squalid' figure in the definitions of most dictionaries – was never very flattering: 'Of uncertain origin', says the OED; of textiles, meaning thin or flimsy; the first example is dated 1670. But there is an even earlier example of its figurative meaning of slight or insubstantial: 'Their vain and sleasy opinions about Religion', from a Civil War publication, *To the High and Honourable Parliament of England, the petitions of some gentlemen of the Easterne Association* (1645).

15 JUNE 1986

Mr Graham Morison, of Paisley in Renfrewshire, sent a handout from a local discotheque headlined: 'Nightclubbing with the fashion pack'. It read, in part, 'Suitable attire: smart, imaginative, trendy, sleasy [obsolete spelling of 'sleazy', says the OED], stylish or fashionable'.

SLIPS of the tongue.

Mr Paul Harvey, of North Molton in Devon, an English language teacher who has specialised in linguistics, has been looking into speech errors. 'They are popular,' he writes, 'both in literature (Mrs Malaprop's "head-strong as an allegory on the banks of the Nile") and in real life. Among others there are "blends" – gristly (grizzly and ghastly); "transpositions" – a cop of cuffee; and "anticipations" – the worst (West) German Chancellor. Spoonerisms are occasionally heard, but I suspect you would have to wait a long time for ones as amusing as some of those attributed to the Rev

W. A. Spooner (1844–1930): "Kinkering congs their titles take", "You have hissed my mystery lectures", "a shoving leopard". Lewis Carroll, much quoted in linguistic literature, has characters who use "errors" – Humpty Dumpty is quick to point out that "slithy" means "slimy" and "lithe". A BBC announcer early one morning produced "No problems reported for ail (rail) or air"; on one TV channel I heard "In Brissels this morning . . . ", on another "binging the brig stars to Los Angeles". Jimmy Tarbuck once asserted that "Brutannia rules the waves". "This is like a Harrer hommer film", a friend said while watching a late-night movie involving a disturbing Australian pseudo-corpse called Patrick. These errors are of interest to linguists because they provide information about the way "chunks" of language are planned in the brain. So next time someone mentions a "carpsihord" or "par cark", remember that strictly speaking it is not a slip of the *tongue*: it's constructive linguistic evidence of a momentary hiccup in what is a highly sophisticated mental process.'

I share Mr Harvey's taste for slips. In my own family I have been reproved for my 'pendantry' (living by the pen as I do, I thought it apt) and for my 'damned condensation'. On Radio 3 earlier this year the composer of *Carmina Burana* was announced as 'Corl . . . ' but with admirable presence of mind (typical of Radio 3), the announcer avoided saying 'Arff'.

30 SEPTEMBER 1984

As I rather hoped, 'slips of the tongue' encouraged readers to send in their own favourites. Here is a selection. 'Several villages are now in Afghan hounds . . . er . . . hands' – Radio 3 some little time after the Russian invasion (from Mr John Neat of Leeds); 'Now let's get down to brass facts' – union official in meeting with civil servants (Mr Philip Jones of Hampton Wick, Surrey); 'My speech is definitely *not* spurred' – granny after a glass of wine at a family celebration (Mrs Rosemary Peacock of Kingsbury, north-west London); 'All our efforts have been fertile' – Yorkshire millworker who, with others, had unsuccessfully tried to rearrange heavy furniture in the millowner's office (Mr Len Atkinson of Shipley, West Yorkshire); 'The Woolworth's Reading is better than the Marlow Reading'; 'Ears have walls'; 'I saw Mrs Dancer Thatching' – Mrs Gillian Goldingham of Maidenhead (sent in by her husband); 'Tonight's Promenade Concert is . . . Verdi's

Montevespers . . . sorry, Monteverdi's Vespers of 1610' – Radio 3 two years ago (Ms Virginia Knight of Mortimer Common, Berkshire). Slips, it occurs to me, are one of the most endearing things about Radio 3.

28 OCTOBER 1984

Still more slips, but they keep coming in. M. R. Wetherfield, of Sutton in Surrey, once heard a reference on Radio 3 to 'Jesu, man of Joy's desiring'. Y. P. Lidell, of Bridgwater in Somerset, writes, 'There are slips of the ear as well as of the tongue. The best example I know concerns my late brother Alvar. One evening before the war, after Alvar had read the five o'clock news, a friend asked him, "What was that in the news about the Navy wanting more fish and chips?" My brother looked up the bulletin and found that in a Parliamentary report a speaker had said, "What the Navy needs is not more ships but more efficient ships".' Paul Jennings tells of a mishearing that concerned his father-in-law, the late Eric Blom, formerly *The Observer*'s music critic. When he died, in 1959, arrangements for the music to be played at his funeral were made by telephone. One of the items asked for was a Bach chorale. What was actually played was the Barcarolle from Offenbach's *Tales of Hoffman*. No one, says Mr Jennings, would have enjoyed the mix-up more than Eric Blom.

11 NOVEMBER 1984

S̲NOOKER TALK. In *Snookered* (Faber and Faber), his crisply written account of the snooker boom, Donald Trelford tells how the game got the name. A newly-joined cadet at the Royal Military Academy at Woolwich ('The Shop') was once known as a 'snooker'. One day in the 1880s, he writes, during a game of what 'had become the favourite variation of billiards of the 11th Devonshire Regiment stationed at Jubbulpore', a young subaltern named Neville Chamberlain (no relation to the Prime Minister) called out to someone who had just missed an easy shot, 'Why, you're a regular snooker!' Years later Chamberlain said that, to soothe feelings, 'I added that we were all snookers at the game, so it would be appropriate to call the game Snooker.' And so it was.

The terminology is packed with metaphor. 'Cue' is from

French *queue*, tail or small end of the mace, as the leather tipped rod was once called. 'Spider', a rest with legs that enable the cue ball to be struck from above when other balls are in the way, comes from an American word for a long-handled frying pan on legs. 'Beginners should be cautioned to watch carefully for foul shots,' says an OED example dated 1896, 'especially when the rest or spider is being used.' Cannon, the billiards shot in which the cue ball hits both the red and the opponent's ball, is, according to the OED, 'also called "carom", of which "cannon" appears to be a perversion'. 'Carom' – which is still the American word for 'cannon' – comes from Spanish *carambola*, a word of Indian origin for a round sour fruit. (Americans also pronounce 'snooker' to rhyme with 'cooker'.)

Incidentally neither Mr Trelford nor I can find how proficiency at snooker came to be associated with 'a misspent youth'.

13 APRIL 1984

My confession of ignorance of how proficiency at snooker came to be associated with a misspent youth did not go unnoticed. Most of the letters referred to the Oxford Dictionary of Quotations, which has, under 'Herbert Spencer (1820–1903)': 'It was remarked to me by the late Mr Charles Roupell . . . that to play billiards [not snooker] was the sign of an ill-spent [not misspent] youth.'

There were variations. Mr Peter Aldersley, Secretary of the Savile Club, writes: 'In the archives of this club it is recorded that Robert Louis Stevenson, who was a member from 1874 to 1894, propounded to Herbert Spencer that "proficiency in this game (note: probably billiards) is a sign of a misspent youth".' (The incident appears in *The Frank Muir Book*, published by Heinemann; Mr Muir too is a member of the club.) The Rev C. F. Warren, of Machen in Gwent, writes that Sir Gurney Benham, in his *Book of Quotations* (1907, revised 1948), has: 'To play billiards well is the sign of a misspent youth.' Mr Bill Comber, of Surbiton in Surrey, found a similar version in Cassell's *Classified Quotations*.

And there were those who explained the expression by recalling billiards and snooker parlours – in particular those to be found above a chain of tailors shops in the 1930s – and the 'layabouts' who frequented them. Some readers said Fifty

Shilling Tailors, others Burtons (then Montague Burton). I had the recollection that there was a single firm called Burton's Fifty Shilling Tailors, but I learn from Mr John Taylor, who edited the *Tailor and Cutter* for 20 years, that there were indeed two chains and that the parlours were above Burtons. FST later became John Colliers – and have now been taken over by Burtons.

4 MAY 1986

SOURCES.

In his memoirs, *The Art of the Possible*, the late Lord Butler tells how he wrote to Churchill when the latter retired as Prime Minister, in 1955: 'We shall miss your strength and sense of direction . . . But this time with you has given me at least the strength to face all things quietly.' He then quotes these lines:

> Let nothing disturb thee,
> Let nothing affright thee,
> All passeth away,
> God alone will stay,
> Patience obtaineth all things.

He adds, 'This, like St Augustine, I have learned.' A tough-minded, useful thought, but the implicit attribution to Augustine worried me and I made desultory inquiries without result – the usual guess was Julian of Norwich, the fourteenth-century anchoress and mystic who wrote: 'All shall be well, and all shall be well, and all manner of things shall be well.' I decided to ask readers if they knew the source, but first I consulted the Rev Dr Huelin, formerly lecturer in liturgy at King's College, London. 'It's St Teresa's Prayer,' he said, 'St Teresa of Avila.' In his biography of her, Stephen Clissold tells of the tense, painful circumstances in which she wrote it. How Butler, with his scrupulous scholarship, misattributed it we don't know; an example, I suppose, of even Homer nodding. (He also omitted the last two lines:

> Who God possesseth, is lacking in nothing,
> God alone sufficeth.

That is my adaptation of two other versions; I am sure Butler would have provided something more elegant.)

Another quotation I have been seeking for years is: 'The Church of England is the Tory Party at prayer' (or words to that effect) – the year does not go by in which I don't have cause to want it. Knowledgeable colleagues on the paper referred me to still more knowledgeable authorities. No luck. I wrote to Lord Blake, whose magisterial works include a life of Disraeli. He told me that a correspondence in *The Times* some years ago had also failed to produce an answer. The quest seems hopeless, but you never know . . .

14 APRIL 1985

Still no luck. There were many suggestions of sources – one as far back as Pitt the Elder; others included Lloyd George and George Bernard Shaw – but very little specific, and what little there was did not stand up to inquiry. I live in hope.

SPONTANEITY.

People are divided about the pronunciation of words ending '-eity', writes Mr Brian Pearce, of New Barnet, Hertfordshire: is it *-eeity* or *-ayity*? So are lexicographers. I have been looking at four such words: 'deity', 'homogeneity', 'simultaneity' and 'spontaneity'. The variations – between dictionaries, between pronunciations in individual dictionaries, between different editions of the same dictionary – are interesting. The OED gives *-eeity* for all four (entries prepared for publication 1894–1914), and in 1981 Dr Robert Burchfield of the Oxford Dictionaries said flatly in his BBC booklet *The Spoken Word* that all such words should be so pronounced. Today, only Chambers agrees. Even the Concise Oxford shows *-ayity* as an alternative in 'deity'; most other dictionaries have it as an alternative in 'spontaneity' too; some have it in all four. Not that Dr Burchfield was unaware of the change that was taking place. Vol. I of A Supplement to the OED (1972) had already noted that 'deity' was 'freq. pronounced' *dayity*, and the forthcoming Vol. IV has a similar note for 'spontaneity'. (I like the variation between the 1976 and 1982 editions of the Concise Oxford: 1976 has '*deeity* . . . or *day-*', 1982 has '*deeity* . . . or D *day-*'. The D, for 'disputed', a new category of 'disputed usage', 'indicates a use that, although widely found, is still the subject of much adverse comment'.

When *-ayity* began to creep in I don't know, but in 1977

Webster's Collegiate – which had already come out in 1965 with *-ayity* as an alternative for 'spontaneity' – did so for all four words. In that year, too, the fourteenth edition of Everyman's English Pronouncing Dictionary, the 'bible' of the pronunciation business, came out showing *-ayity* as an alternative for 'deity' and 'spontaneity'. Still more significantly, it indicated that in the latter, the editor of the dictionary, the late A. C. Gimson, had judged that *-eeity*, 'although widely used', was 'somewhat less common' than *-ayity*. Could it be that *-eeity* is on the way out for all '-eity' words?

28 JULY 1985

S==TATE OF THE ART, writes Mr Stanley Sharpless, of Christchurch in Dorset, 'seems to be the current buzz-phrase'. He quotes a British Telecom advertisement: 'We're also responsible for . . . a host of other state-of-the-art innovations.' When, he asks, 'did this curious phrase originate? And what does it mean?'

I too thought it a recent expression and so did half-a-dozen people I asked. However . . . Volume IV of A Supplement to the Oxford English Dictionary defines it: 'the current stage of development of a practical or technological subject; frequently (especially in attributive use) implying the use of the latest techniques in a product'. The first example reads: 'It has therefore been thought desirable to gather under one cover the most important papers . . . In the present state of the art this is all that can be done' – H. H. Supplee, *Gas Turbine* (1910). But the entry also refers to 'status' in the main dictionary, which has the example: 'The illustrations give a good idea of the present status of the art in the various methods of printing' – *Anthony's Photographic Bulletin*, 1889.

27 JULY 1986

San Francisco

DEAR MR SILVERLIGHT, *I was interested to read your report on 'state of the art', but disappointed not to find any discussion of the point that has always interested me. That is, when it changed from a noun phrase, as in the earlier example you quoted, to an adjectival phrase – apparently a synonym for up-to-date, modern, or technically advanced – as in the later example. The former usage seems to me entirely unexceptionable, while the latter seems, as they used to say on Monty Python, distinctly silly.*

I first saw the phrase used in its adjectival sense, complete with hyphens, in an advertisement in the American magazine Science *in the early 1960s.*

Yours

Michael V. Mahoney

Manchester

Involved as I am in the high-technology world (I am in the computer industry), I am bombarded with the expression 'state of the art', and I have come to believe that it is misunderstood by most copywriters. To describe a product as such is to indicate what is known and accepted by all practitioners in the field, that it is tried and tested; the expression has to do with consolidation of knowledge. Many advertisers, however, use it to suggest innovation and the pushing forward of the frontiers of science, the opposite of the meaning I understand. Nearly every day I make choices between a product which works well but may be long in the tooth (state of the art) and one which promises greater benefits but uses a less well-tested technique (innovation). It would be a pity to lose the distinction.

Regards

Phil Cantor

After reading those two letters I noticed that the makers of my typewriter claim that it 'marks a revolutionary new addition to our product line-up, incorporating state-of-the-art electronic technology'. Recent examples in the files of the Oxford English Dictionaries show the expression being used predominantly in this sense. The writing, I fear, is on the wall for the earlier sense. This radical change in usage is adumbrated in the definition in Volume IV of A Supplement to the Oxford English Dictionary but is not noted in so many words, and I failed to point it up in my piece. This has now been done by Mr Mahoney and Mr Cantor. Mr Snape, in his letter below,

110

shows that the expression was in use half a century earlier than was previously thought. And, of course, it was Mr Sharpless's letter that prompted the exercise in the first place. Altogether it aptly illustrates the part in the workings of the column played by readers of *The Observer*.

Preston

DEAR MR SILVERLIGHT, *It so happens that I came across the expression 'state of the art' in a much earlier publication that the OED's example. It was bound in with the* Journal of the Royal Agricultural Society, *and I enclose a photocopy.*

Yours sincerely

ROBERT SNAPE
Librarian, Lancashire College of Agriculture

The photocopy was of advertisements from the *Royal Agricultural Advertiser*. One, for the five-volume *Farmers' Ladies' Library of Rural and Household Economy*, Volume III, *Domestic Cookery*, reads:

> Suited to the present advanced state of the Art, but founded upon Principles of Economy and Practical Knowledge. By Mrs Rundell. *Sixty-seventh edition*. Improved by the addition of 900 New Receipts, and a Chapter on Indian Cookery. Fcap. 8vo., 6s. *Of this Volume upwards of 280,000 have been sold.*

S══════════════════════════════════

STYLE. The *Financial Times* has brought out a new internal style book. Its appearance was marked one day last month by an article on the centre pages, along with others on such matters as South Africa, the tin crisis and Mr Janos Kadar's visit to this country. Here was striking evidence of the paper's serious approach to usage. I have been allowed to look at the book and am impressed – a better word might be shamed – to find, after 35 years in the game, how much it taught me. I liked the note on 'none' (about which I have tangled with readers): 'usually singular, but sense may sometimes require a plural verb – none but the brave are likely to succeed'.

In the article the News Editor, David Walker, says the book

111

'is the result of many months of work by senior journalists'. No doubt. From my own experience I also have no doubt that arguments were frequent and vehement. My pet cause on *The Observer* over the years has been the plural of 'Germany', East and West. I advocated 'Germanies' – as in the Kingdom of the Two Sicilies, the only historical analogy I could think of. It is a lost cause. The paper's style is 'Germanys'. Mr Walker is modest about his craft but proud of it too: 'The concept of the newspaper as a guardian of the language is not one to strike a responsive chord in the world outside journalism'. The word 'journalese', he agreed, had some justification. 'Yet, with no French-style Academy to worry about the shape and direction of language, English is heavily dependent on the press for the way in which it is used and develops. The internal style book represents our answer to that challenge. In it reporters are reminded that to anticipate marriage is a very different thing from expecting it, that stockbrokers have to be leaping out of upper-floor windows as the market collapses before a recession becomes a slump, that hopefully describes a state of mind rather than meaning it is hoped, and that hike should be restricted to a description of a long walk.' (Mr Walker also gave a pat on the head to journalists who write about words.)

I would go further on the importance of the press. Some of the best writers I know have been proud to call themselves journalists. Some of the best writing in the kingdom appears in newspapers.

1 DECEMBER 1985

Cyril Ray (who once began an article in the *Spectator* condemning hypocritical Welsh religiosity: 'Speaking as a Celt – my maternal grandfather was a rabbi in Cardiff . . . ') writes: 'In the late 1940s I was invited by its old comrades' association to write the wartime history of 78 Division which – as a *Manchester Guardian* war correspondent – I had seen in action throughout the Italian campaign. Three major-generals who in turn had commanded the division were asked to form an editorial committee, simply to act as administrators; it was agreed that I should submit my MS to them only for the correction of factual errors – I was given complete editorial freedom. But I had written of an infantry company's realising, after wading a river waist-deep, that they had "bitten off more than they could chew". My MS came back with the phrase

112

crossed out; the word "Journalese!" in the margin; and the generals' preference: "encountered stiffer resistance than they had anticipated". I would not have thought that I could ever win an argument against even one major-general, let alone three, but I did – even if the whole passage had to be cut in the end because of space.'

(When I wrote in my piece that some of the best writers I know are proud to call themselves journalists, Mr Ray was one I had in mind.)

2 FEBRUARY 1986

TART.

Mona Williams of Bampton, Oxon., writes: 'I am convinced I know the origin of the term "tart". Fifty years ago a Cockney child would say, "My bruvver is out wiv' 'is tart", the word being an abbreviation of "sweet'art". It would really be an endearment. Since then the word has had a descent comparable to Lucifer's.'

Old memories stirred. As a young officer just before World War II, I heard agonised gunners protest, 'But Sarge, I *can't* go on guard duty tonight, I'm going out with my tart', and sometimes it worked. When I expressed surprise that having a date with a prostitute could get someone out of guard duty I was told that 'tart' only meant girlfriend ('chaste or not', as an OED example has it). None of my younger colleagues on *The Observer* have heard of this non-derogatory usage; among older ones, only those brought up in or near London's East End know of it, and they agree it is now obsolete.

Partridge has some interesting references under 'tart'. One is ' . . . a term of approval applied by the London lower orders to a young woman for whom some affection is felt' (from an 1864 slang dictionary). Quoting another source, he says ' . . . by 1904 only of fast or immoral women', which is at odds with Ms Williams's and my experience. Another Partridge definition is 'The young favourite of one of the older boys; not necessarily a catamite: Scottish Public Schools: C.20 (Ian Miller, *School Tie*, 1935).' Last week the *Sun* reported that 'hard-porn games featuring explicit sex are being played on school computers. A floppy disk of five filthy all-colour games is now circulating in

113

schools.' One is entitled *Tart*. The word's descent is indeed almost comparable to Lucifer's.

Letters from all over the kingdom take me to task for giving the impression that the use of 'tart' in the non-derogatory sense of girlfriend was confined to London. Here are excerpts from some of them: '"Tart" was in common use among working-class boys here [Edinburgh] from the mid-1930s to about 1950 without a pejorative sense. I'd say that even now tart-prostitute is not much heard and is regarded as rather English. We stick wi' hures . . . ' (Mr Stuart Harris). 'In our boyish circles in Sydney, where I lived up to the age of 10, "tart" was the word for a girl. Eric Partridge's Scottish public school example applied at my school in England too' (Mr John Wilson, of Beckington in Somerset). 'You will be pleased to know that "tart", applied to respectable girls, is still current in the Irish Guards – a regiment that is "50 per cent Ulster, 50 per cent Eire and 50 per cent Liverpool, sir!" as my first platoon sergeant put it' (Major S. J. L. Roberts, 1st Battalion, Irish Guards). 'In the North-East the term has always been derogatory. I still retain a sense of indignation at the slap I received when a child for innocently reporting to my mother that one neighbour had called another a "right tart". At eight years old, I considered that a compliment since it meant for me a delicious piece of confectionery' (Maureen Brook, Morpeth, Northumberland).

There was also mention of a similar use of 'bird'. Mr George Gould, of Billericay in Essex, writes that in the East End of London the word formerly 'would only be applied to a prostitute. Nowadays it has the same non-derogatory sense as "tart" used to have'. 'A maiden, girl' is one of the first definitions of 'bird' in the OED; an example dated 'after 1300' reads, '[Mary] that blisful bird of grace', from *Cursor Mundi, The Cursor* [i.e. *The Messenger]* o *the World*. Volume I of A Supplement to the OED has, referring to that definition, 'In modern, revived use, a girl, woman, often used familiarly or disparagingly'. Partridge (1984) has 'a girl, since *ca.* 1880; a sweetheart, military, since *ca.* 1890; a harlot, since *ca.* 1900, but now obsolete in this nuance', which bears out Mr Gould's recollection. 'The sense sweetheart, or simply girl, had by 1920 become fairly general, although still uncultured. Since then it has worked its way up the social scale to arrive near the top, in

114

the late 1960s, in the term "dollybird".' This term, defined as 'a sexually attractive, usually young and pretty, girl', says Paul Beale, who edited this latest edition of Partridge, 'belongs particularly to the brief era of the mini-skirt'.

Mrs Jane Ladyman of Exeter, going off at a tangent, as she says herself, writes: 'I recently came across "fanny" in the Penguin English Dictionary. It merely said, "Fanny – arse". Looking at the compilers, I found that the editor, Professor Garmondsway, had spent some time in Canada [which would explain the milder, American sense of the word]. I wonder what he would have made of the old last war joke. Winston Churchill, having been told that one of his cleaners has a daughter in the Army, sees her scrubbing the doorstep of No. 10 as he goes out. "Ah, good morning, Gladys. And how long has your Fanny been at the Front?" "Only about half as long as your arse has been at the back".' My amusement at the joke was tempered by a touch of ruefulness. When I came to this country as a child most of my Americanisms – sidewalk, elevator, automobile, ashcan, etc., etc., etc. – were laughed out of me. For some reason 'fanny' wasn't. In my late teens or early twenties, desperately trying to acquire some social graces, I was at some function (a tennis club dance, I think). Telling a no doubt boring anecdote, I said, 'I fell flat on my fanny.' I still remember the horror when someone drew me on one side and explained the sudden icy silence that greeted my remark.

30 DECEMBER 1984

TOUGH IT.

The writer and former diplomat Sir James Cable wrote in *Encounter* last November that the Argentines 'must either take an initiative . . . capable of breaking the emotional deadlock [on the Falklands], or they must tough it out'. I first heard 'tough it out' after Watergate: Julie Nixon said in 1974 that her father would 'tough out the impeachment process to the end' – *Newsweek*, quoted in the forthcoming Volume IV of A Supplement to the OED. However, the Supplement also has this example from the *Massachusetts Spy*, 1830: 'Judy, with whom he had toughed it three years'. The first BrE example quoted is: 'Fraser [then Australian Prime Minister] will tough out this latest crisis' (*Observer*, 15 April 1981).

26 MAY 1985

DEAR MR SILVERLIGHT, *Just prior to reading your column on 'Tough it' I had discovered the following from the novel* The Country of the Pointed Firs, *by Sarah Orne Jewitt, first published in 1896, 'There ain't nobody here but me . . . I'd rather tough it out alone.'*

Yours sincerely

ANN BADHAM

DEAR MR SILVERLIGHT, *'From now on the kidnappers must tough it out alone', from Brian Moore,* The Revolution Script, *first published in the USA 1971 (Penguin 1973). This example is from Moore's documentary novel about the James Cross kidnapping in Montreal in 1970, and is even more interesting because Moore quotes the French Canadian version:* 'Mais, maintenant, il faut le tougher. Le tougher *is a French Canadian coinage, another dogsbody word adopted from English. It means to endure, to survive the blows. It describes a condition which French Canadians have been forced to cultivate. From now on the kidnappers must tough it out alone.'*

Yours sincerely

JOHN COLLINS

T RILLION. On 7 June the *Standard*, reporting on 'America's ballooning budget deficit', wrote that Federal Government spending last year was 'running at $1.5 trillion a year . . . (A trillion has 12 noughts.)' Twelve? Surely a trillion is a million times a million times a million: eighteen noughts. Then I remembered how in 1974 Mr Callaghan, then Prime Minister, had given his blessing in a parliamentary answer to the American billion (nine noughts) against ours (twelve noughts).

The struggle has been going on for some time. According to the OED, two Frenchmen of the late 1400s and early 1500s, N. Chuquet and Etienne de la Roche, explained billion, trillion etc. as 'successive powers of a million [i.e. six noughts for each jump], the trillion being the third power of a million . . . as always used in England'. Then, in the mid-1600s, the 'erroneous custom' was established in France of 'calling a thousand millions a billion and a million millions a trillion, an entire perversion of the nomenclature of Chuquet and de la Roche, an error unfortunately followed by some in the US'. Unfortunately or not, the Americans seem to be winning. Trillion with twelve noughts, says the forthcoming Vol. IV of A Supplement to the OED, 'is increasingly common in British usage'. (Incidentally, a centillion, a million to the power of 100, has – English style – 600 noughts, which would fill some ten or twelve of these lines.)

17 JUNE 1984

Professor Robin Harte of Cork University's Mathematics Department writes: 'Your American trillion prompts me to advocate the Irish thousand, which may amuse you by its presumption. Our thousand is one hundred hundred (10 000) compared with the British and American thousand, which is ten hundred. The Irish thousand would give an Irish billion of ten to the power of sixteen (10 000 000 000 000 000), which the Americans would have to call 10 quadrillion. By the time we in Ireland have used up one new word, therefore, the Americans will have used up three, and be well on their way to a fourth.'

1 JULY 1984

T ROUBLESOME WORDS. What is wrong with this sentence: 'Indonesia intends to double its exports of liquified gas to Japan'? Five out of five colleagues failed to spot the error: 'liquefy' has only one 'i'. The word appears in the new *Dictionary of Troublesome Words* by Bill Bryson (Allen Lane and Penguin) and I have an uneasy feeling that if I had been asked to spell it before reading the book I would have got it wrong. Mr Bryson, who was born in the United States in 1951, is a deputy chief sub-editor on *The Times* and cheerfully quotes his own paper along with others, including *The Observer*, for examples of abusage; eminent authorities, living and dead – the revered Fowler himself – are not spared. My favourite entry (speaking as someone who has been censured for confusing the two words) is 'shall and will'. 'Even in England,' it says, 'the distinctions are quickly fading and are by no means fixed.'

I have queries. 'Holocaust is not just any disaster, but one involving fiery destruction.' As Mr Bryson says, the word in Greek means 'burnt whole', but long before the Holocaust of the Second World War its sense had been extended to destruction on a vast scale, not necessarily by fire. 'Kith and Kin . . . together are redundant and hackneyed.' Hackneyed perhaps, not entirely redundant. According to Mr Bryson's own entry 'kin' are relatives, 'kith' are acquaintances and relatives. Anyway, doesn't more than 500 years of usage justify the expression? The OED's first example is, 'Fer fro kitth and fro kynne' – Langland's *Piers Plowman* (1377). 'Shambles . . . as a serious and considered term is otiose when there is no connotation of slaughter.' 'Shambles' did indeed once mean slaughterhouse, but for more than half a century most people have taken it to mean utter confusion – with no connotation of bloodshed. But all that is niggling. The book is a good deal more useful than most recent products of the ever-expanding English Usage industry that I have seen – and a good deal cheaper too.

29 APRIL 1984

TRYST.

In his *Observer* television column last month, Julian Barnes wrote of a character in the series *Marriage* who, among other things, 'was meant to go to a rugger international, slyly tryst with an old girl-friend, do the naughties practically on camera, get found out . . . '. All very eye-catching – even if, as the article made clear, 'it was all tamer than this' – especially that word 'tryst'. Not a word people use much – but perfect in that context. The Longman Dictionary of Contemporary English (*Eldoce*, as it is called in the trade), which is aimed primarily at foreign English speakers, defines a tryst as 'an arrangement between lovers to meet at a secret place or time' (Pyramus and Thisbe in *A Midsummer Night's Dream* come to mind: 'Wilt thou at Ninny's tomb meet me straightaway?'). I know of no other definition that so concisely and comprehensively conveys the word's overtones. More interesting still was Mr Barnes's use of 'tryst' as a verb. One of the gravest offences in the eyes of readers who complain to us about what they

118

consider bad writing is what one correspondent, commenting on my defence of 'to target' (see RUBBISH), described as 'the sloppy practice, mainly by journalists, of using nouns as verbs'. It was, he said, 'to be deplored'. I can only plead that the practice is as old as the language. (The OED's first example of 'to target', incidentally, is dated 1837.)

In the OED's entry 'house', the second example with the word as a noun is dated 1000 (the earliest is from *Beowulf*, probably written about the end of the seventh century); so is an example with 'house' as a verb. Examples of 'harbour' both as noun and verb go back to 1150, of 'tryst' to 1375. A quotation from *Legends of the Saints in the Scottish Dialect of the Fourteenth Century* reads (slightly modernised): 'She kepyt the trist . . . and with her brocht the man on hy, Quhare she tristit prively.'

2 MARCH 1986

Belfast

DEAR MR SILVERLIGHT, *'Tryst' is still in common use in Ulster, particularly in the more 'Scottish' areas, like mid-Antrim. There it is used for an appointment, an agreement to meet – usually to make a deal about cattle. For example you'll get a farmer downing his glass and saying, 'I'm for off – I'm trysted to see Wullie-John at the back of four about a wee heifer he has.' In fact Chambers (so authoritative on Scots words) gives 'cattle-fair' as one of the meanings of 'tryst'. Incidentally the word is always pronounced to rhyme with 'Christ', never to rhyme with 'mist'. The first time I heard the English pronunciation I thought the speaker was away in the head. Kissed in a tryst? No, spliced in a tryst!*

Sincerely

M. GRANT CORMACK

Dundee

DEAR MR SILVERLIGHT, *I remember that when I was a schoolboy in the mid-1940s, living in Larbett, in Stirlingshire, the local annual fair was called the 'Tryst'. This had had its origin in a cattle market, but had become a carnival and fun fair. The OED has the example, 'The two great annual markets for black cattle, called the Trysts of Falkirk' (1776, Nimmo,* A General History of Stirlingshire). *The word was used by Sir Walter Scott, not least in* The Two Drovers.

Yours sincerely

GORDON J. H. PONT

Northampton

DEAR MR SILVERLIGHT, *Fifty years ago at school we studied* Lays of Ancient Rome, *by Macaulay:*

> *By the nine gods he swore it,*
> *And named a trysting day, etc., etc.*

We all thought of a tryst as a lovers' meeting, but our schoolmaster told us it was any *prearranged meeting.*

Yours sincerely

L. W. CLARKE

An impressive array of information. Variations in approach to the word between dictionaries, even between different editions of the same dictionary, are interesting. The OED entry, ready for publication in 1915, shows it pronounced with a long 'i' and derived from Old French *triste*, 'appointed station in hunting'; it adds, 'The sense sometimes corresponds with that of "truce".' There are six definitions of the noun, seven of the verb, though the differences are too slight for them to need quoting in full. They are adequately summarised in the modern Concise Oxford as: '1 (noun) appointed meeting, appointment . . . 2 (verb transitive) engage to meet (person), appoint (time, place). 3 (verb intransitive) make a tryst (with).' As will be noted it is all very neutral; nothing romantic here. No guide to pronunciation is offered. The Shorter Oxford (1933) has short 'i' first, long second; the 1933 Concise has diacritical marks above the 'i', with the mark for short on top (˘), from which I assume that short 'i' is preferred.

Among OED examples, I like this one, dated 1375, from John Barbour's *The Bruce* (*The Acts and Life of the Most Victorious Conquerour, Robert Bruce, King of Scotland*):

The kyng . . . richt toward the houss is gane
Quhar he set trist to mete his men.

(Barbour, *c.* 1320–95, is described in the *Oxford Companion to English Literature* as 'a Scottish poet, archdeacon of Aberdeen and one of the auditors of the exchequer in 1357, 1382 and 1384'. The *Legends of the Saints* quoted in the 'tryst' piece above has also been attributed to him, says Margaret Drabble, the editor of the *Companion* – it is 'certainly from Barbour's period and area of origin' – but she adds that that is disputed.) As for 'romantic' examples, the only specific one is, '1844, Mrs Browning, *Brown Rosary*, "Now where is Onora?" . . . "At the tryst with her lover".' Others that may be romantic are

An' she has put on her net-silk hose,
An' awa to the tryste has gane

(1700) from *Remains of Nithsdale and Galloway Song* by Robert H. Cromek; 'Their tryst in the wood' (1859) from Meredith's *The Ordeal of Richard Feverell*; and 'She stood . . . keeping her tryst at the stile' (1878) from *On Seaboard*, by Susan Phillips.

Chambers shows the word pronounced with long 'i'; it describes its use as 'chiefly Scot.'. Collins, like the rest of my desk dictionaries, shows both short and long 'i', with short first. The first definition is 'an appointment to meet, esp. secretly'. Neither Chambers nor Collins give any romantic connotations. As someone who grew up in North America, I am tempted to think they come from there. Dictionaries that emphasise them are either American (e.g. Webster's Collegiate; 'an agreement, as between lovers to meet') or have American links. Longman, which produces *Eldoce*, has access to the data base assembled by Merriam-Webster, which produces the Collegiate. The Reader's Digest Great Illustrated ('An agreement between lovers to meet at a certain place or time') was 'adapted and developed from the lexical database of the Houghton Mifflin Company of Boston Massachusetts'. However, Lesley Burnett of the Oxford English Dictionaries – who was educated in Scotland – agrees that those romantic connotations are what first come to mind in modern usage. There is also that letter from L. W. Clarke, who, while at school in this country in the 1930s, 'thought of a tryst as a lovers' meeting'. Volume IV of A Supplement to the OED has no entry for 'tryst' so for the moment we have no authoritative explanation of when they came in or from where. Perhaps

121

Mrs Burnett, who is revising the Shorter Oxford, will provide one.

WHO/WHOM. Mr. H. B. Collier of Edmonton, Alberta,

writes: 'There seems to be an epidemic of "whom" among journalists – "whom" as the subject of a verb.' He quotes an *Observer* profile, 'whomsoever has been elected leader of the party' and, from a Canadian paper, 'the man whom the policeman said was running down the road'.

Not just among journalists and not just in our time. The Authorised Version has Jesus asking his disciples, 'But whom say ye that I am?' (Matthew 16:15). In *The Tempest* Prospero speaks of 'Young Ferdinand, – whom they suppose is drown'd.' Then there is 'who' for 'whom'. Fowler quotes: 'When the Queen asks her retiring Prime Minister about who she should summon to head the government, he wants to offer her an unequivocal answer' and, 'Before the intrusion of television into politics, politicians knew pretty well who they were speaking at.' It is one of the abiding difficulties in the English language which people have always been nervous of; another is 'I/me', which I wrote about some time ago and provoked a storm of abuse by saying that even though I knew it was 'incorrect', I preferred 'older than me' to 'older than I'. There are those who would simply abandon 'whom'. It could happen. Professor John Honey, of Leicester Polytechnic, said in a letter apropos the 'I/me' controversy: 'One can perhaps foresee a time when we will abandon differences of pronoun case just as we have abandoned the case of nouns.' Someone once wrote a letter to *The Times*: 'Surely the word "whom" is now a pretentious archaicism', and gave this account of a telephone conversation: 'To whom am I speaking?' 'Sorry, wrong number. No one we know says "whom".' Last month the poetry critic of the highly literate *Listener* wrote in a review, 'who are you talking to', and I saw nothing wrong with it – indeed, I cannot remember when I last used 'whom'.

And yet . . . 'for who the bell tolls'? And what about 'Who whom?' Lenin's brilliant, brutally succinct summary of how he saw the realities of political power?

23 FEBRUARY 1986

DEAR MR SILVERLIGHT, *Please allow me to comment on your remark that although you knew it was incorrect, you preferred 'older than me' to 'older than I'. The form preferred by you is not incorrect at all. It is not a question of different 'cases', but of the use of the emphatic form 'me' instead of the unemphatic 'I'. The French use the* je/moi *to make the emphasis clear. The answer to the question 'Who's there' – 'It's us' – is not 'incorrect': 'It's we' is just impossible in idiomatic English. 'It's I' may be possible, but the more idiomatic form would be 'It's me'. Formal – often called 'logical' – criteria have to give way to 'psychological' criteria which make up a language. The sentence you quote, 'who are you talking to' (and naturally you agree with its use) again is 'correct'. The who is part of an elliptic sentence 'Who is it you are talking to' or something similar. Ellipses are used in many languages and lead to 'incorrect' collocation in the eyes of those who are linguistically naive. School grammars deal with only a small part of the language inventory; their aim is to be normative (and rightly so) to prevent the train from getting off the rails. However, there are more ways of locomotion.*

Sincerely

GIDEON COHEN

That letter was a rare exception to the almost entirely critical response to 'who/whom'. Another was from Mr Alec Bristow, of Eye in Suffolk, author of the letter to *The Times* quoted in the piece, who commented on the reference to Donne: 'When Donne's *Devotions* appeared in 1624, English was a much more inflected language than it is today. The passage containing the words "for whom the bell tolls" continues, "It tolls for thee." I suggest that, while the final accusative pronoun is more obviously obsolete because of the demise of the old second person singular, the preceding one is now just as dead for everyone except a dwindling number of people who wish to show off their grammatical superiority. That does not mean that when we quote from Donne we should attempt to alter his words in line with present English usage (which would, I suppose, produce not "for who the bell tolls" but "who the bell tolls for"). Surely nobody would wish to rewrite our authors of past centuries; often their archaic language emphasises their timelessness and places them beyond the vagaries of fashion. But that does not mean that they should be copied today; genuine old half-timbering may have dignity and charm, but fake half-timbering is corrupt.'

On Lenin's 'Who whom?' Mr C. M. Woodhouse wrote: 'Although it was Lenin who made it famous, it was not original. It is a quotation from Gogol's *The Government Inspector*, Act IV, Scene 8, final line, *Posmotrim, kto kogo!* – 'We shall see – who whom!' (The 'g' in the quotation, I am told, is pronounced 'v'.)

X

X. The letter 'e' I believe, occurs more than any other in the alphabet – I counted sixteen appearances in two lines of a biography pulled at random from my bookshelves; 'a', with nine, came second; 'r' and 't' both had eight; 'x' did not appear on the page at all. 'C' has a whole OED volume to itself, 's' has two volumes, 2306 pages. 'X' has seven pages. So much for statistics. 'X' has qualities all its own. It is the great unknown, thanks to Descartes who, in his *Géometrie* (1637), used 'z', 'y' and 'x' as symbols of unknowns corresponding to the symbols 'a', 'b' and 'c' of knowns. Where would journalists be without 'Mr X' and 'Miss X'? But 'x' has a deeper potency. It corresponds, says the OED, in form and position in the alphabet, to the Greek *chi*, as in *chaos*, or *chronos*, or, most potent of all in our civilisation, *Christos*, 'the Anointed One', as the lexicon has it (from the verb meaning to anoint), 'the "Christ", as a translation of the Hebrew "Messiah"'. The first example of 'X' as an abbreviation for 'Christ' is dated 1100. The next, dated 1380, is from a sermon by Wycliffe: 'X bitokeneth Crist'. So to 'Xmas'. 'This is a spelling of "Christmas" rather than a synonym for it', says the Longman Dictionary of the English Language. 'It should be confined to commercial and casual writing.' The OED's first example is dated 1551: 'From X'tenmas next following.' Coleridge wrote to Southey, 'My Xtmas Carol is a quaint performance' (1799). On 6 December 1884 *Punch* had: 'He's beginning Xmassing already.' The OED doesn't offer a pronunciation. Longman, after giving *eksmas*, says, 'Most people prefer to say *Christmas* rather than *eksmas* when reading it aloud.' Chambers and Collins give *eksmas*, *krismas*, Webster vice versa. The Shorter Oxford says roundly, 'Sometimes vulgarly pronounced *eksmas*', and the Concise, in keeping with that sentiment, has only *krismas*.

Y UPPIE. Once upon a time there was the 'hippie', defined by Volume II of A Supplement to the OED as 'a hipster; a person, usually exotically dressed, who is, or is taken to be given to the use of hallucinogenic drugs; a beatnik'. The first example is dated 1953; another, from the *Daily Telegraph*, reads: 'These people, "writers, musicians, psychedelic popsters and hippies . . . " see London as a "focal city for permissive experiments" in art and life' (21 February 1967). Then came the politically active hippie, the yippie, a member of the Youth International Party: on 15 October 1970 *The Observer* carried the headline 'Yippies go home', referring to the expulsion from this country of the Yippie leader Jerry Rubin. So, in the Reagan Age, to the yuppie, young, upwardly mobile professional, with its faintly contemptuous echo of yippie and puppy. Julian Barnes wrote in *The Observer* in August of 'yuppie' estates in Dallas. There is a slight awkwardness about the definition: 'yuppie' has no 'm' (for 'mobile') and some Americans use 'yumpie', as in a piece in the *Wall Street Journal* of 13 August by Herbert Stein, former economic adviser to Presidents Nixon and Ford. In the same article Mr Stein describes himself as a 'grumpie', one of the grown-up, mature people; he also writes: 'George Will [right-wing columnist who has been credited with the coining of 'yuppie'] is too young to be a real grumpie, but I would nominate him for honorary membership.' It's probably all rather ephemeral, but I like the fact that the man who seemed to be the archetypal yippie, Jerry Rubin, now in his forties, is a Wall Street tycoon, the typical yuppie in fact.

Another word readers are asking about is 'preppy' or 'preppie', pupil (or pertaining to one) at an American preparatory school. Again it is usually contemptuous, as indicated in the first example in Vol. III of A Supplement to the OED: '"Preppy", silly, immature' (1900). The schools could be described as a cross between our sixth-form colleges and more exclusive 'public' schools. Two well known ones are Groton (pronounced *grotton*; F. D. R. went there) and Choate (J. F. K.).

Mr Mike Taylorson of Hartlepool writes that on the same afternoon as reading that piece, with its note expressing unease about the definition of 'yuppie' (the alternative spelling) thanks to its lack of an 'm' for 'mobile', he heard the word on Radio 3. Philip French, *The Observer*'s film critic, was interviewing the American critic Richard Grenier, who defined 'yuppie' as 'young urban professional': 'upwardly mobile' is the source of a similar Americanism, 'yumpie'. I asked Our Man in Washington, Robert Chesshyre, about the expression. He writes: 'The "urban" in "yuppie" is a vital part of the definition. The group so designated, comprising the affluent offspring of the baby-boom generation (born 1946–1964), have rejected the suburban dreams of their parents and would feel spiritually deprived if they were not within jogging distance of a *brie*-selling delicatessen. They gentrify downtown row [AmE for terrace] houses, and – in addition to their high-paying jobs – plunge into enterprises that are possible only in cities. They were the backbone of Gary Hart's short crusade for the US presidency, but they switched happily to vote for Reagan, whose supply-side economic theory dignifies their relentless acquisitiveness as something more noble than simple greed. Yuppies not only want it all but have the skills and drive to get it. I have heard quite serious talk about "getting by on $100,000 a year" – by no means an unusual figure for a childless yuppie couple. Keeping fit is an article of faith: a beautiful body is the foremost cherished possession. Eating gourmet food is a close second. A Texan girl described her moment of apotheosis when she opened a yuppie friend's fridge during a visit to Washington: "I saw things the names of which I didn't know. It was my first exposure to the expanded experiences of the planet."'

A crisp account with more information than anything I have yet read on the subject.

5 MAY 1985

Had I read the *Economist* of 17 March 1984, quoted in Volume IV of A Supplement to the OED, all would have been made clear: 'Mr Hart seems to have drawn much of his support from young, upwardly mobile people and young urban professionals, yumps and yuppies as they are called.' I don't really regret not having done so. It was a roundabout way to arrive at the answer, but an interesting one.